YOUNG
Revolutionaries
WHO ROCK

AN INSIDER'S GUIDE
TO SAVING THE WORLD
ONE
REVOLUTION AT A TIME

Dallas Jessup
with Rusty Fischer

sutton hart press
PORTLAND, OREGON

SUTTON HART PRESS

www.suttonhart.com

LIBRARY OF CONGRESS CATALOGING-IN-PUBLICATION DATA

Jessup, Dallas, 1991-
Fisher, Rusty, 19xx
Young Revolutionaries Who Rock / Dallas Jessup and Rusty Fisher
– 1st ed.
p. cm.

PRODUCED AND PRINTED IN THE UNITED STATES OF AMERICA
ISBN: 978-0-9815027-7-9

BOOK DESIGN: M. Warren

DEDICATION

This book is dedicated to the dream that every girl should be able to go anywhere she wants without fear; to the brave ones who have survived the unimaginable; and to the families that have endured rape, abduction or abuse.

This book is dedicated to the schools that teach girls how to fight back; to the organizations that have incorporated *Just Yell Fire* into their program; to the law enforcement agencies that have embraced *Just Yell Fire*; and to the girls who have shared the film with their friends.

This book is dedicated to the thousands of kids who have decided that now is the time to make a difference and who will begin to do what it takes to save the world today.

ACKNOWLEDGMENTS

I am so blessed to have such talented and generous people around me.

I would like to thank my parents, Jay and Maggie Jessup, who have been there through it all. They have encouraged me and supported me in countless ways. I want to thank them for listening to me and for always letting me know that anything is possible and I can do it.

Rusty Fischer for listening to me, helping me to write this book using my voice and never treating me like a kid. Andy Mingo, my editor, for seeing my vision and making it better.

Thank you to the staff and teachers at St. Mary's Academy in Portland, Oregon, who worked tirelessly around my insane travel/speaking schedule so I wouldn't miss out on the great education they deliver.

This book wouldn't have been possible without the following people, for whose help I am grateful beyond words: Lorraine Elias, an absolute master at graphics, Master Anthony Neal, who taught me to never give up, no matter how much it hurt. Evangeline Lilly and Josh Holloway, for selflessly loaning their celebrity to a kid so that girls everywhere would be safer, *Do Something!*, for the encouragement and support they have given me and many of the others Revolutionaries mentioned in this book. Sutton Hart Press, for believing in me, in my cause, and for taking a chance on a teenager. Chad Von Dette of VIPER Academy, for teaching me to fight like a girl, InNate Graphics, for countless hours of tech support and so much talent. Platform Strategy, for taking me on and making sure the world knows about *Just Yell Fire*.

And thank you everyone who has enabled the *Just Yell Fire* project to teach a million girls around the world that they have rights and exactly how to stand up for them: Takafumi Uehara, Integra Telecom, Google, Ed Henry, Rick Lord, Deborah Anderson, Clackamas Community College, Park Maguire, Brian Martinek, and everyone who worked on the movie set and backed us in everything we have done.

A huge thank you to the Oregon FBI and Special Agent Sandra Flint. They have encouraged, inspired, and helped me to get the word out and they have helped us with the tools we needed to get it right.

I would like to thank the Huetteman family, Anabel Wirth, the Wadzita family, the South family, the Frazier family, the Gist family, Shirley Janney, Dr. Frank McCoy, Dr. Glenora McCoy, Anita Bingham, the Sevy family, Kathy McDonald, Tony Alfiere. They cheered me on, kept me grounded and always let me know they were proud of me.

Thank you to Vasanth Kuppuswamy and his family for their hard work and welcoming hospitality during my speaking tour in India.

A very special thank you to the incredible rock band, Enation, for standing by me, believing in me, and donating their song *Permission to Dream* to *Just Yell Fire* so that we can send more DVDs to girls around the world.

Finally, thank you to some amazing friends who are always there to remind me what's important and what isn't, and to laugh with me along this incredible path: Sophie Gist, Emily Sevy, and Jamie Frazier for being The Most Amazing

Friends. No matter what is going on in my life they never treat me any differently, always make me laugh, and share my happiness in all the good things that have happened.

x

GL Girl's Life Magazine | February/March 2008 Issue

Fight Plan

Dallas Jessup, 16, had lots of motivation when she took up tae kwon do at age 15: "My dad had told me I couldn't date until I had a black belt." All that training paid off as she produced her movie Just Yell Fire after seeing the abduction of 11-year-old Carlie Brucia that was captured on security videotape. "At the same time, there were several abductions and attempted abductions in Portland, Ore., where I go to high school. My friends were asking me what they could do to protect themselves because I have a tae kwon do black belt and am a certified instructor in Filipino street fighting. I decided to make a home movie showing some moves for my friends, but the project took on a life of its own." Soon, she had a volunteer professional crew of 30, and Lost stars Evangeline Lilly and Josh Holloway even agreed to do cameos. To date, more than 325,000 girls at schools, shelters and police agencies in over 37 countries have seen the film, available for free through download or DVD. To check it out or to learn more, go to justyellfire.com. And for more from our interview with this kick butt teen, go to girlslife.com

Justine Magazine | June 1, 2007

Get Fired Up!

When Dallas Jessup was 14, she saw the scary real-life footage of a local teenage girl being abducted in her hometown. And since the security tape was constantly running on the local news, Dallas couldn't get the images out of her head. "She was a girl at that time, about my age, and she just went away with a guy willingly," Dallas remembers. Four days later, the same girl was found dead.

Sadly, over the next few weeks, there were numerous additional abductions, and after more research, Dallas found that one in four girls are date raped before they graduate college. "It was so alarming to hear," she says. "I go to an all-girls school of about 600, so knowing that 150 of them could be date raped, that's just terrible. My friends started coming to me, going, 'What do we do?' so I decided I wanted to help." Armed with tons of support, a black belt in Filipino martial arts and certification in tae kwon do, Dallas set out to make a difference.

Dallas learned up with her friend Catherine, whose mom worked at a community college. Catherine's mom hooked them up with some people skilled in film production who were more than thrilled to help the girls with their project.

Even big stars, like Lost's Evangeline Lilly and Josh Holloway, hopped on board. "Catherine's cousin works on the set of Lost, so we asked him to help us get a celebrity endorsement," she remembers. "Teens are so highly influenced by celebrities, so we thought it would help to reach a wider audience." Evangeline and Josh were game to shoot cameos.

Before Dallas knew it, Just Yell Fire was born. "The name 'Just Yell Fire' came from Chad Von Dette," she explains. "When he was little his dad told him to yell 'Fire!' because people will look to your direction."

Dallas knows that gut feelings are way more important than most people realize.

Although Dallas originally started the project with hopes of keeping her friends safe, she's now focused on empowering girls all over the world.

Now that the video is available to everyone as a free download at justyellfire.com, Dallas's main goal is spreading the word.

Dallas's wish is paying off.

People Magazine | April 16, 2007 Issue

She gives girls the power to stand up – and fight back

Moment of Truth: In February 2004, Dallas saw a TV news clip of a security video in which 11-year-old Carlie Brucia of Sarasota, Fla. was led away from a car wash by Joseph P. Smith, who was later convicted of her rape and murder. "It was so chilling," Dallas recalls. "I thought, 'This could happen to my best friend.'"

So Dallas, who holds a black belt in tae kwon do and is certified in Filipino street fighting, recruited friend Catherine Wehage, 16, as well as a self-defense instructor and a video director to make a movie showing girls "how to put up a fight."

Big Results: Since it debuted online last October at justyellfire.com, Just Yell Fire - named for the phrase Dallas suggests victims should shout to draw a crowd - has been downloaded over 100,000 times and viewed in 34 countries. In it, Dallas demonstrates self-defense moves like eye-gouging, ear-pulling and groin-snapping - all vetted by a martial arts pro and designed to enable a woman to escape from a much larger attacker. (And thanks to a lucky Hollywood connection - Catherine's cousin works on the set of Lost - Evangeline Lilly and Josh Holloway make cameos.) Dallas's message has struck a chord with girls like Courtney Connell, 18, who wishes she had known how to defend herself when an ex-boyfriend attacked her several years ago. "I was panicked, hyperventilating," recalls Connell. "I'd never thought something like this would happen to me."

Caring Award winners push the limit of reaching out
By Svetlana Shkolnikova, USA TODAY

Dallas Jessup, 16, raised $500,000 from donations to produce Just Yell Fire, a film she wrote to teach girls how to protect themselves in times of danger. Two million people in 37 countries have viewed the film.

Those who seek inspiration need look no further than the winners of this year's National Caring Awards. Ten recipients, five adults and five young people, were honored by the Caring Institute Monday night in Washington, D.C., for their service to charitable causes and for setting an example for others.

Founder and director Val Halamandaris created the awards in 1989 after reading Mother Teresa of Calcutta, who he says worked him to do something about "the poverty of the spirit in America." The Caring Institute was founded to promote the values of caring, integrity and public service. Winners were selected from a pool of 25,000 nominees by the Institute's Board of Trustees.

Past honorees include former president Jimmy Carter and his wife, Rosalynn, chimpanzee researcher Jane Goodall and baseball Hall of Famer and community volunteer Cal Ripken Jr.

This year's winners "are proof that one person can make a difference," Halamandaris says. "They show that there really isn't any limit to what you can do if you believe in it."

TABLE OF CONTENTS

Dallas at the Frederick Douglass Hall of Fame where she was inducted into the Hall of Fame for Caring Americans

INTRODUCTION

Welcome
to the Revolution!

"Never doubt that a small group of thoughtful, committed citizens can change the world. Indeed, it's the only thing that ever has."

—MARGARET MEAD

Americans love a good Revolution. In fact, Thomas Jefferson once said, "A little rebellion now and then is a good thing."

Maybe one starts with dumping tea in a harbor to start a Revolution for Freedom; perhaps another starts with an inspiring speech, challenging the citizens of a great nation to judge people by the content of their character and not the color of their skin in a Revolution for Civil Rights; and just maybe a new revolutionary change in the world starts today in this library, in this study, in this living room, in this cozy chair by the window – with you reading this book, one page at a time.

Revolutions, after all, aren't always fought by large armies or entire nations. They don't even require gunfire, violence or bloodshed. In fact, the most important revolutions start small; one person at a time. An idea, an observation, a thought or even just a feeling can all give rise to the power of a revolution.

That's why I'm here: I want to challenge you to start a Revolution of your own and to let you know just how to make that happen. Anybody can be the catalyst for a fundamental change in our society, even kids.

The younger you are, the more power you actually have to act on your thoughts, feelings and emotions. Think about it: you grow up, get married, buy a house, have kids of your own, and get bogged down with bills and responsibilities. How are you going to start a revolution then? We have the freedom, the power, the energy, the dreams and the courage to start revolutions. All we need is a little push. I've met about 100 kids that have done just that with 100 separate causes and I've heard about 1,000 more, and that doesn't include the few 1,000 I haven't *heard* about.

If you'll join us, I think we'll see a very different and far better world five years from now; a better world created by Revolutionaries like *you* and *me*.

YOU HAVE THE RIGHT TO TAKE BACK YOUR POWER

Since I started the *Just Yell Fire* Revolution a few years ago, I've met a lot of rape survivors and near-rape avoiders. They've all told me horror stories that I hope you never have to hear or experience. And the one thing all rape victims – all victims in general – have in common is a feeling of powerlessness. Whether it is by surrendering your power unwillingly, the taking of your power without permission, or purely a lack of personal power, being victimized is a horrible feeling.

Do you know how that feels? I bet you do. Kids are some of the most powerless people on the planet; or so we think. When you are bullied and afraid to leave the house, that's powerlessness. When you are singled out because of your race, religion or sexual orientation, that's powerlessness. When you are punished by parents, principals and the powers that be, that is powerlessness in its simplest form.

When you can't play on this team because you're a girl or cheer on that squad because you're a boy, that's the powerlessness of inequality. When you can't walk to school because bigger kids might hurt you, that's the powerlessness of injustice. When you turn on the evening news and see hunger and earthquakes and tornadoes and hurricanes and bombings and are frustrated by the inability to help – *that's* powerlessness pure and simple.

But I want you to know that you can turn that powerlessness around and into real positive power; many a revolution began by turning powerlessness into power.

When settlers braved hunger and thirst and wild animals to colonize America, they did so because they felt powerless back home in England. When England began persecuting settlers all over again in their new country, they felt powerless once more. They were tired of feeling powerless and so they did what no one thought they could do: they started a revolution.

I'm here to tell you that you don't have to be powerless anymore.

It's time for you to take back your power.

It's time for your Revolution!

You Have the Right to Be a Revolutionary

When I first saw the video footage of eleven-year-old Carlie Brucia being abducted in front of a carwash in broad daylight several years ago, I was outraged. When I learned that Carlie had been raped and killed, I was sickened. When her killer was put in jail, I felt that Carlie had been vindicated. That feeling lasted only a moment, and I only felt slightly satisfied.

I knew that a woman is raped every two minutes in the United States. I knew that there are over 114,000 attempted abductions every year. I knew there would be more Carlies later that day, and the next, and so on and forever. But I knew something else: I knew I had the right to try and stop it. I knew I was powerful enough to overcome these feelings of powerlessness.

I knew I could start a Revolution of my own; I just had to figure out *how*.

So I started the *Just Yell Fire* movement and made a film about how to avoid being abducted or raped – and as of this writing 600,000 people have downloaded it from every corner of the world. I started speaking at schools all over the United States, and now I operate the *Just Yell Fire* non-profit organization, which has helped empower girls in 41 countries.

But what about *you*?

What can *you* do to turn your anger into action? What are *you* concerned about that you care enough to start a Revolution? What can *you* do to start changing the world, one kid at a time?

I'm here to let you know that you have rights. Maybe you don't possess the right to vote or the right to drive or drink alcohol... *yet*. But here's a list of 9 rights that every one of you already has – even if you've forgotten what they are:

YOU HAVE THE RIGHT TO...

- Get Angry at Injustice
- Live a Life Free of Fear
- Believe in Yourself
- Fix What's Broken
- Listen to Your Gut
- Change the World
- Help Others Who Can't Help Themselves
- Fight for Your Rights and the Rights of Others
- Fight for Your Personal Bill of Rights

I'm here to remind you of the rights you have and don't use, as well as the rights you may not have even realized you had in the first place. I'm here to remind you that if you do not protect these rights, you may very well lose them.

I'm here to let you know it's time for you to start saving the world, one Revolution at a time.

YOU HAVE THE RIGHT TO RECOGNIZE YOUR POWER – AND USE IT!

Here's the kind of real, usable power I'm talking about: you are school-smart and you know something of how the world works and how to use technology in order to reach hundreds, even thousands, of people with a single Facebook post or YouTube video or text message – and even with all that knowledge racked up in your brain **you have power you don't even know about**.

You have the power to start a Revolution – a Revolution where not only *your* life gets better, but hundreds or thousands or even millions of people improve the quality of their lives, too. You can be more than just a kid or a jock or a nerd or a brain or a cheerleader or whatever label the world uses to describe you now; *you* can be more than that.

You can be a Revolutionary!

Let me tell you about a world I've discovered and one you can be part of: when *Just Yell Fire* took off and hundreds, then thousands, then millions of people joined my revolution to put predators and rapists out of commission worldwide, I was amazed at this unprecedented response to my cause. Because of all that activity, I received hundreds of invitations to meetings around the country. These meetings are usually centered on an award or scholarship for community service, but what they are really about is bringing kids together who are trying to change the world. It's a way for all of us young revolutionaries to meet and greet; to get a break from school and work and fundraisers and catch up with each other – or meet each other for the very first time.

It's really amazing to sit in a room with other kids who have made a difference in the world and talk about things like cancer cures and eliminating homelessness and poverty and quitting smoking and getting relief for flood victims. These kids are just like you and me and they have actually solved these problems in their own communities. We're not just talking pie-in-the-sky theories or warm and fuzzy wannabes; these are **Young Revolutionaries Who Rock**!

In just the past couple of years I've become part of this brave new world and have met some phenomenal people along the way:

- I met a guy from Canada who was bullied by kids and even bullied by his TEACHERS when he was growing up because he was different from them. He started an organization to teach people tolerance. He soon had 300 people working for him and has a million others helping him now – he is a Revolutionary.

- I met a high school student from South Carolina who found out about a school in India without books, without desks and without electricity. He called companies around the US, and now spends his summers delivering container loads of supplies to this school and others like it in India – he is a Revolutionary.

▪ One girl figured out how to communicate with autistic kids. She's spreading the word, and parents, doctors, and teachers all over the world are listening – she is a Revolutionary.

▪ One girl sent a few CDs and DVDs to the troops overseas. The response she got was so overwhelming that she started a non-profit organization to encourage other people to provide more gifts for soldiers – she is a Revolutionary.

And I have hundreds of stories just like these, stories of modern revolutionaries who couldn't wait any longer and decided to *fight for their right to a better world.*

Kids are taking on world hunger, speeding up the search for cures to horrible diseases and standing up for the environment. We are teaching other kids about the dangers of smoking, the effects of drugs, and the problem of underage drinking. We are doing what adults can't, won't, or just plain don't. So there are thousands of kids changing the world – all different colors and shapes and sizes and zip codes – and do you know what they all have in common?

They all started out in middle school or in high school. Most weren't old enough to drive; they had never given a speech or held a public office; they weren't the best students or the best athletes; they were just everyday, normal, average kids. Kids like me, kids like you. But the other thing they had in common was that they all saw a problem and decided to do something about it. They went from being kids to becoming **Young Revolutionaries Who Rock**.

Young Revolutionaries Who Rock don't wear uniforms or pick up guns. They don't fire bullets or tear down walls.

They simply see something that needs fixing and fix it – or at least are in the *process of fixing it*. They don't wait around for help or ask the government for assistance or pass around petitions; they woke up one day, took a step in a new direction and started their own personal revolution to change the world.

And THAT is what this book is about. In these pages you will find everything you need to know about how to spot a problem, find a solution and then share it with the world, one revolution at a time.

That's all you have to do:

- Spot a problem
- Find a solution
- Share it with the world

So here is the part of the book where the author would typically say that you should find your passion. I want to challenge you in a different way.

So, let me put it in a way any young revolutionary can appreciate:

YOU HAVE THE RIGHT TO GET ANGRY

I'm angry that thousands of guys are abducting girls and raping them, killing them or selling them into slavery; that's MY thing. But what makes YOU angry?

Do you get angry when you see your friends getting bullied?

Do you get angry when you see companies pouring toxic waste into the rivers and streams of our country?

Do you get angry knowing that someone has a disease that they are denied the cure for because they don't have ENOUGH MONEY?!

Do you get angry knowing that 1 in 5 kids in our country go to bed hungry? Imagine what THAT feels like.

Well then, stop wasting your energy on anger and start putting an end to the bullying, the polluting, or hunger. Stop putting it off and find a way to get food to those kids or CDs to the troops or money to those in need or to solve whatever problem you want to take on. *No matter how old you are, you are old enough to know what makes YOU angry and to do something about it.*

It's easy to feel powerless in the face of so much hunger, poverty, sickness, crime, violence, bloodshed and scandal that we see on the news every day. But revolutions are about taking back your power and doing something about it.

Are you ready for that?

I have a feeling you *are* ready – right now, *today*. I have a feeling you picked up this book because you didn't just want to know what **Young Revolutionaries Who Rock** look like but because you wanted to become one yourself. Well, now is your time; here are all the tools you'll need in one handy resource and all that's left for you to do is to make the decision.

It's time to start your Revolution.

You Have the Right to be a Young Revolutionary Who Rocks

In this book you will meet 9 amazing kids – just like you – who saw a problem, decided to fix it, and started their own revolution from the ground up. They aren't millionaires, they aren't politicians' kids or celebrities; they're just normal kids who wanted to right a wrong and knew the only way to get it done was to start a revolution. So they did.

And here are the **Young Revolutionaries Who Rock**:

Vasanth Kuppuswamy... who turned a summer trip to his father's village in India into a nonprofit organization that provides education, supplies, motivation and inspiration for children to complete school and go on to college.

Claire Crawford... who started a program to give teddy bears with cleft palates to children with cleft palates so they won't feel so alone in the hospital as they recover from surgery.

Chad Bullock... who has made it his life's mission to stop kids from smoking – and make sure other kids never start.

Ana Dodson... who started an organization called *Peruvian Hearts* when she was only eleven to improve the quality of life for children in Peru who are living in orphanages or in extreme poverty.

Daniel Feldman... who started the non-profit organization *Kids Feeding Kids* and has raised nearly $40,000 by organizing bake sales and other fund-raising activities to feed hungry children.

Niha Jain... who visited a local battered womens' shelter and was so moved that she started an organization called *Generation United to Succeed (GUTS)* to help fund women's shelters in her community and make them a more pleasant, inviting place to go in time of need.

Pat Pedraja... who, while recovering from chemotherapy for cancer, saw a news story about how hard it is for minorities to get bone marrow transplants and started an organization to help them do just that.

Austin Gutwein... who helped bring the plight of children orphaned by AIDS in Africa to light when he went to his school gym and shot 2,057 free throws to represent the number of kids who would lose their parents during the average school day. Not only did Austin raise awareness about the desperation and devastation that AIDS was causing in Africa, but he raised money to help with every single basket!

Jeremy Dias... who, when bullied by classmates (and even teachers) for being "colored and gay," successfully sued his school board – and used the award money to create a youth-driven charity to address discrimination and promote diversity in Canada's communities and schools.

Jasmine Petro... who, in addition to her own charitable work, teaches other kids how to be **Young Revolutionaries Who Rock**!

But guess what? With all the great, passionate, inspiring young people you'll meet in this book, there's still one missing. Can you guess who it is? That's right, it's *you*. You may not know one single, solitary thing about India, bone marrow transplants, the negative effects of nicotine, the poor people of Peru, cleft palates or even shooting baskets, but deep down inside I *know* you have something to contribute, something to give, something that sees a need for change.

This is your chance to join the revolution.

This is your chance to be one of the **Young Revolutionaries Who Rock**!

YOU HAVE THE RIGHT TO MEET MENTORS WHO ROCK

Nancy Lublin

What if you could start a revolution where women who are down on their luck could have access to the same business attire that wealthy women wear? What if you could recycle business suits that some women were no longer wearing and give them to other women who really, *really* needed them to find – and keep – professional jobs?

That's exactly what Nancy Lublin did in 1996, when she inherited $5,000 from her great-grandfather, Poppy

Max. According to *DressforSuccess.org*: "Nancy wanted to honor her grandfather's memory and legacy by using his hard-earned money to help other people blaze new beginnings."

"A law student and new to New York City, Nancy turned to some experts for help; she established the organization with three nuns from Spanish Harlem who each ran public service programs. Together, they built *Dress for Success* New York into a vibrant organization serving women from all over the city and boroughs."

"The mission of *Dress for Success* is to promote the economic independence of disadvantaged women by providing professional attire, a network of support and the career development tools to help women thrive in work and in life."

"Founded in New York City in 1997, *Dress for Success* is an international not-for-profit organization offering services designed to help our clients find jobs and remain employed. Each *Dress for Success* client receives one suit when she has a job interview and can return for a second suit or separates when she finds work. By fall of 1998, there were nearly 20 *Dress for Success* programs. A year later there were close to 50 *Dress for Success* affiliates in three countries."

Later Nancy became CEO and, as she's known around the office, "Chief Old Person" at the great human rights organization *DoSomething.org*. As it says on their website: "*DoSomething* believes you have the power to make a difference. It is our aim to inspire, support and celebrate a generation of doers: people who see the need to do something, believe in their ability to get it done, and then take action. At *DoSomething.org* we provide the tools and resources for you to convert your ideas and energy into positive action. Be part of a generation of doers."

Now, I don't want this book to be about adults, but I didn't think it would hurt to hear from **just one very special person**, either. And when I found out about all she's done for kids, I thought Nancy Lublin was the perfect adult to be my official **Mentor Who Rocks**! I interviewed Nancy for this book and wanted to share some of what she said with you, because more than anything I could say right now I think Nancy Lublin speaks to the heart of being a **Young Revolutionary Who Rocks**.

Before she became one of the hardest working "volunteers" in the country, Nancy Lublin was like a lot of hardworking twenty-somethings: attending law school and trying to make her parents proud. But she might have lost herself in the process. Recalls Nancy: "I hated law school. From the first minute, I was miserable. It was such a hostile, competitive environment and everyone just cared about getting ahead, being on law review, getting a great (i.e. high-paying) job. I really wanted to use the law as a weapon for social change. One day I came home from class to find a check for $5,000 from the estate of my great-grandfather – the person in my family who came here with nothing and worked hard his whole life (practically every family has a hero like this...). And I thought, what do I do with HIS money? Spontaneously the idea for *Dress for Success* came to me – and I went to work on it right away (I think because it was also a terrific way to procrastinate and avoid law school homework)."

After her success with *Dress for Success*, Nancy was brought in to turn things around at *DoSomething.org*. She explains: "When I arrived here, there was $75,000 in the bank, they had just laid off 21 or 22 people and all the office materials were in storage in Queens. This has been a turnaround. We now have 15 full-time people and about 6 paid interns and an operating budget of over 3 million dollars cash a year – more importantly, we now reach millions of young people."

It was a hard job, but somebody had to do it. Nancy believed that "somebody" was her; she still does. What does Nancy love most about her job? "I believe in what I do!" she says. "I actually care about the people and our product!"

I asked Nancy what advice she might have for today's youth and (not surprisingly) she has some great advice: "Don't wait," she cautions. "You don't have to be Bono or Bill Gates to make a difference."

But her best advice might be just a little more practical: "I have two ears and one mouth for a reason: I should listen 66% of the time."

xxix

Now, here's the thing about Nancy: she loves **Young Revolutionaries Who Rock**! She was eager to be a part of this project because she works with young people every single day and truly wants them to succeed. And you know what? So do most adults you'll meet along the way. So when you're in need, or even just in doubt along the path to your very own revolution, don't be afraid to find a **Mentor Who Rocks**.

YOU HAVE THE RIGHT TO GET ACTIVE: PARTING GIFTS FOR THE REVOLUTIONARY

I know how kids think. Well, actually, how *all* of us think. We want to know: What's in it for me? What do I get out of this? And that's okay. There's lots in it for you and let me tell you about what you get when you start your own personal revolution.

You get two "parting gifts" when you become a Revolutionary:

Parting Gift # 1:
Extracurricular to the Nth Degree

First, let me tell you about the insanely cool things that I get to do and that these 1,000 kids I've told you about are also experiencing:

Over the past year I've been flown to New York and Washington, DC, at least a dozen times for awards and to spread my message on television shows. I've been on *Good Morning America*, *Montel Williams*, *Fox News Live*, *The Today Show*, *CNN*, and many more. The producers send you plane tickets, your own limo, put you up in hot suites at cool hotels, and the works – just for being a **Young Revolutionary Who Rocks**! Nice!

People, *Teen*, *Justine*, *Seventeen*, *ElleGirl* and a bunch of other magazines did photo shoots with me and/or ran feature articles. My picture was on the huge teletron screen in Times Square; three senators have brought me to their offices in DC to brief them on *Just Yell Fire*, **AND** get this: last September I was featured on 25 MILLION Doritos bags – just for being a **Young Revolutionary Who Rocks**!

I went to Texas to give a speech, Oregon the week after and, at a Womens' Conference in New Mexico, I was the featured speaker next to Mia Tyler, Steven Tyler's daughter and a sister revolutionary herself – and all this while I'm still going to school. Teachers are backing my play and let me out of school for a day or two about every other week. I email my assignments and my friends cover for me in classes.

xxx

Top: Dallas and Josh Holloway of *LOST*; Josh starred in *Just Yell Fire*. Bottom: with Senator Bob Dole

Teen Choice Awards in Los Angeles. Top: Dallas and Britany Snow. Bottom: with Zac Efron, from *High School Musical*

I went to India for two weeks during the summer of 2008. You're reading this book because a publisher heard about what I'd been doing for the last two years and offered me a book deal on the spot. To top it all off, I was nominated for a *Teen Choice Award*! I was flown to Hollywood, and stayed at a very cool hotel on the Hollywood Boulevard where they threw a pre-party for us at a hot night club. I walked the red carpet with major celebrities and partied all night with Jesse McCartney, JoJo, Lauren Conrad, Diamond Dallas, Danika, Shailene Woodley, and many others.

Then, the next night at the *Teen Choice Awards*, I walked the red carpet again. I hung out in the Green Room and met Josh Holloway, Brittany Snow, Penn Badgley, Brenda Song, Selena Gomez, Zac Efron, and Vanessa Hudgens. I was treated as an equal and at the awards ceremony I was seated in the second row right behind Hayden Panettiere and Will Smith. How cool is that?

All that just for being a **Young Revolutionary Who Rocks**!

And these are just a few of the things you get for making a difference in the world. BUT remember I said you get two things for starting a revolution and the second thing is more important and much more valuable to me: Best Friends Forever.

Parting Gift # 2:
Friends to the Nth Degree

Young Revolutionaries hear from the people who have been helped by their work. I mean, these are people you've never met before, oftentimes who live on the other side of the country – or halfway around the world – who have had their lives impacted by **something you've done**. Can you imagine anything cooler on this planet than helping a complete stranger change his or her life?

My best moment wasn't hearing that I'm a finalist for some big award; it was hearing from a 13-year-old girl in Los Angeles who **saved her own life** using one of the techniques we show in the *Just Yell Fire* film.

My best moments over the past year weren't the CNN Hero feature or an all-expenses-paid trip to the nation's shopping capitols (although both were pretty darn cool, don't get me wrong). No, the best moments were the "thank you" notes and emails I got from all over the world. There is nothing more moving than having a mother thank you for saving the life of her child or having a girl come up after a *Just Yell Fire* presentation and thanking me for letting her know there is something she can do to stop being abused at home.

It was a great feeling having 500 important people cheering when I received the *Caring Award* in Washington, DC. But it was much more moving to read just one email: a girl I've never met said she had avoided abduction by using my technique but that her friend, who didn't know about *Just Yell Fire*, was abducted and killed.

These are the kinds of moments you will get to experience, cry over and cherish – that's your ultimate reward for being a **Young Revolutionary Who Rocks**. And that's why I'm asking you to decide what makes you angry and to do something about it – and here's how you start:

YOU HAVE THE RIGHT TO FIGHT FOR YOUR PERSONAL BILL OF RIGHTS!

Right about now you might be thinking to yourself: "Man, Dallas, this all sounds great…but how do I get started?" Don't worry; there are hundreds of ways you can start being more active in your community – *today*.

Start where you spend most of your time – at school. Once you see the problem you want to solve – otherwise known as the Revolution you want to start – go to your teacher and let him or her know you want to do an extra credit project. (Teachers love this stuff, so I promise they'll help you.) This way you can learn as much as you can about world hunger, a fatal disease or an environmental problem.

Give a presentation to your class on your findings. (Believe me, it's good practice for when you're on television or speaking in front of 200 Middle School girls who walk into the room with attitudes.) Start an action committee and call the local newspaper to let them know what you're doing.

What happens next – and it sounds so simple but it's absolutely, positively 100% true – is that people start calling you to **find out how they can help**. That's where the Revolution kicks in: from your idea, your actions, the ball starts rolling and soon other people join in to help keep it rolling.

Because, you know what? Deep down, most people really are good. We all want the same things in life – good food, nice clothes, and a comfortable place to live – and we all want to do more, know more, and help more. And it is my feeling that most people – like you – want to give more. Sometimes we just don't know how. So when someone like you or me or the awesome people you'll meet in this book get the ball rolling, well, that's usually all it takes.

Of course, you're the main "go to" person. After all, this is YOUR Revolution! You can't do it all but the idea and taking that first step is what starts everything. Lawyers, media people, fundraisers and organizations all want to help a kid who is doing something important.

That person could – and should – be *you*.

Don't wait another minute for someone to come to your rescue, or sign your petition to pass a bill twenty years from now. Don't be the person who sits on the sidelines while everyone else makes way for change. Don't be the person who waits too long to step in and intervene and cause change to happen.

Start a Revolution of your own – *today*. It starts in your bedroom, at the library computer, before or after school; it starts today and it starts with you. One year from now I want to be getting text messages from you saying, "OMG – now it's me. I'm feeding the hungry, I'm fighting for a cancer cure," or whatever your cause.

I hope to see you guys in DC, New York City, or in *Teen Magazine*. Thanks for listening, thanks for reading and thanks for taking this journey. So if you're ready, your "Bill of Rights" awaits.

■

You have the power to start a Revolution where not only your life gets better, but hundreds or thousands or even millions of people improve their lives, too. You can be more than just a kid or a student or a jock or a nerd or a brain or a cheerleader or whatever label the world uses to describe you now. You can be more than that: you can be a **Young Revolutionary Who Rocks**!

■

"You can't change everything," Dallas knows, "but you can change the one thing that is really on your heart."
— Dallas Jessup

Dallas being inducted to the Frederick Douglass Hall of Fame for Caring Americans in Washington, DC

Part One
GET ANGRY

Dallas with students at a school in Maganurpatti,
Tamil Nadu, India

CHAPTER ONE
I Have the Right
to Get Angry at Injustice

"Changing the world doesn't have to be in a far-off place like India; there is need right in your own backyard. Go fix those problems. Pick a project that you're passionate about and get to work to fix the problem. The change will come naturally."

—VASANTH KUPPUSWAMY, Age 19

We know this much: EVERY Revolution starts with some kind of injustice. Whether it's England wanting to exert more pressure over colonists in America or me wanting to tell girls how to avoid becoming another horrible statistic of sexual abuse, injustice is the seed from which every Revolution grows.

So, what does injustice look like to you?

Does it look like a smaller kid being bullied by a bigger kid? Adults having all the rights and kids having none? Teachers making the rules and not listening to their students, even when their students make sense? Real children going hungry while companies waste millions of dollars producing so-called reality shows?

Maybe injustice looks a lot like the neighborhood where you live, where you don't feel safe walking to school or going out after dark. Or maybe injustice looks like that long line of kids waiting to get their free lunches – and sometimes even free breakfasts – every day. Or maybe, just maybe, injustice looks like something that happened to you.

To me, when I discovered that "I Have the Right to Get Angry at Injustice," injustice looked like grown men preying on teenaged girls and 114,000 attempted abductions each year. It looked like a system where the odds were stacked against us and girls weren't taught self-defense in schools or rec centers or youth clubs or the Girl Scouts. But this isn't about me; this is about you. This is about the feeling deep in your heart that you know something isn't right.

Maybe you live in a poor community where kids at your school need all kinds of help. Maybe you've got a friend who's in trouble or a neighbor who might lose their house because of the mortgage crisis or a buddy who can't afford to fill up his car to get to work because of the gas crisis. All of these unfortunate instances are examples of injustice. Good people losing ground to bad people, bad timing, bad situations, bad decisions or just plain bad luck. What can you do to help?

Definitely something.

Anything…

Your first step is to take action. Nothing – and I mean absolutely nothing – gets done in this world without taking that first step. Think of where we'd be if Bill Gates hadn't taken that first step to create better, faster, more affordable home computers. Think of where our country would be if Martin Luther King, Jr. hadn't been a civil rights revolutionary.

Every Revolution starts with that first step; every Revolution requires action.

WHAT ACTION LOOKS LIKE

Sometimes I'll catch myself sitting backstage before a speech or a presentation actively listening to the person introducing me. I have to admit that I don't always tune in to this part of the speech because I've heard it a few hundred times before, but every once in a while I'll pay attention to the presenter reeling off all of my "accomplishments": activist, actor, screenwriter, producer, Teen Choice Nominee, CNN Hero, trainer, martial arts expert, coach… whatever.

And I smile and think, "If he only knew…"

If he only knew that I'd never acted before I stepped onto the set of the *Just Yell Fire* film production. If he only knew that the closest thing to a script I'd ever written before was a grocery list or a text message to my friends. If he only knew the silly mistakes and jitters I had before I became a "producer" for the very first time.

My point is, before I became an actress-slash-screenwriter-slash-producer I didn't know how to make a self defense film and hand it out to nearly 1 million girls in less than a year; I just knew that girls were being attacked in record numbers and I had to do something about it. All I knew was that I had to act. I also knew that girls like me would watch a video and learn from it rather than taking a class or going to a gym. I knew it would be easier for girls to download the video from the Internet anonymously, rather than going down to Blockbuster and renting it in front of all of their friends.

I knew that a lot of girls can't afford to buy or even rent a DVD or they don't have a credit card to pay shipping and handling, but they are scared and want to know what to do and so a FREE video would be the answer.

But I did not know how to go from what I knew to what I needed to get done. Where could I find the cameras to make the video? And who would hold them and who would call the shots and how long would it take and, good gracious, how much would all this *cost*?

I didn't know all that; I just knew I had to act.

3

So I talked to some people who knew more than I did about films and cameras and screenplays and websites and DVDs and downloads. I told them what I wanted to do, told them why and then, more importantly, I asked them for help.

I overcame my natural shyness – yes, believe it or not I'm incredibly, absolutely SHY – and bugged everybody I ever knew who had ever taken a picture, let alone held a movie camera.

It wasn't easy, but I did it. I could have easily given up; many times I wanted to give up. But my anger and sadness and fear for what was happening to girls my age all over this country made me get out of my comfort zone, clear my throat, speak up and speak out. I just had to do it; I didn't have a choice anymore. So I started talking to adults, found that many professionals in the film industry were interested in helping my cause, and asked them to volunteer their time to help make the film.

Amazingly, it all worked out. And better than I ever could have expected.

That's what action *looks* like; that's what action *feels* like.

If I had actually sat down and thought about what I was going to do – the website, the schools, the speeches, the questions, the answers, the nervousness, the shyness, the fundraising, the video, the traveling, the expenses – I might not have ever tried to do anything at all. But then I thought of the abduction and murder of little Carlie Brucia and knew I had to do something; I'd work out the challenges one at a time.

I learned to A.C.T. now, think later.

A.C.T. Now, Think Later

When you find something that makes you angry, or a charity to raise money for, or a cause to champion, it's important to plan, to outline, to make sure that what you're doing is a.) Feasible b.) Legal c.) Helpful. This takes a little work.

4

Scratch that; it takes a LOT of work. There are forms to fill out and people to meet and phone calls to make and messages to leave and emails to read and lots of i's to dot and t's to cross. (But it's all worth it!)

It also takes a lot of action.

And, as we all know, action starts with A.C.T.

A IS FOR ASK

It's okay if you don't know how to start your own personal revolution. After all, we're still kids. What the heck do we know, right? Whenever I meet someone who's done something amazing, I always ask them how they got started. Usually, the first thing they say is, "I asked a few adults first."

Funny, that's just what I did!

Almost every one of the thirty crew members who worked on the *Just Yell Fire* video was an experienced, talented, wise and professional adult. From the director to the sound guy to the guys who rigged the lighting, they had all done this hundreds of times before; that's why the end result looked so professional and first-rate.

I could have done it all myself, sure, and it would have looked exactly like what it would have been: a homemade video by a girl with good intentions but NO movie-making skills whatsoever. Instead I talked to my parents and my trainer and my friends, and they talked to this guy and that lady and this man and that woman, and eventually we had enough people surrounding us who knew what they were doing to get the job done right.

But what is really cool is that Clackamas Community College let their film students help as camera grips – and whatever else we needed – and they actually got school credit for working on the film!

5

That's another amazing thing about wanting to help others: the help comes back to you in droves. People really do want to get involved, so the minute they hear of a worthy cause they're eager to jump in and help – like those film students at the community college. I was worried they'd be too busy or too cool or too offended that we couldn't afford to pay them, but my fears were ungrounded. In fact, just the opposite was true: they leaped at the chance to work on a real movie, the school credit was just a bonus for them. These students got to work with real professionals on a real film, so they were happy to do it. I still get emails from some of them who are using their experience on the *Just Yell Fire* set as a major element of their resumes in search of work on other films. (Not bad for a high school freshman with just an idea.) That's my point: don't be afraid to ask adults and mentors and older kids for help, but use that help to advance your revolution.

6

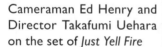
Cameraman Ed Henry and Director Takafumi Uehara on the set of *Just Yell Fire*

So what about you? Let's say you want to do something revolutionary like start a book club for underprivileged kids. Where do you start? Where do the books come from? Where do you store them? Where will you find the money to put them up in a storage shed or box them up or put them into categories? What if the response is overwhelming and you have to rent two storage sheds? What if the response is underwhelming and you have to go out and hunt down more books just to get started? Can you do it all yourself? Won't you need help?

I can tell you from experience that fighting injustice is very time consuming and, as we all know, there are only so many hours in a day. There are meetings and organization and planning sessions and going here and going there – all the while you're still going to school and trying to have a social life. And what if you're dating someone special or involved in athletics or some other major after-school activity?

So you will need help and plenty of it, but how will you get it? You ask for help, that's how. You get your friends, your family, your neighbors, your boyfriend or girlfriend or teammates or classmates involved. And the nice thing I've found is that people of all ages, not just young people, are more than willing to help you.

Here are just a few of the categories of people you can call on for help when you start feeling overwhelmed:

- Classmates
- Neighbors
- Friends
- Family
- Teammates
- Volunteers
- Your parents' friends
- Church members
- Youth group acquaintances
- Girl Scouts / Boy Scouts
- 4-H Clubs
- Elected Officials
- Teachers

7

C IS FOR COMMITMENT

Changing the world takes commitment; just ask anybody who's ever tried. Sometimes I'd love to stay home on a weekend and just chill with my friends, hanging out at the coffee shop or the beach or just listening to tunes in my room, but there's always another training session to teach or another group of girls to inspire or another email newsletter to write or speech to memorize or plane to catch.

Not that I'm complaining; I have the best "job" in the world and there's nothing else I'd rather be doing. I just don't want you to be surprised when you start your very own revolution and suddenly you're the most popular kid, or at least best known on your block! It can take some getting used to.

And you know what? It's a lot like running or working out or eating right or shopping for clothes that fit; it's part of my life now. Once I'm there and speaking and the girls are smiling and laughing and moving and kicking and learning self-defense, there's nowhere else in the world I'd rather be.

But it's not always easy at first, so fair warning: fighting injustice takes commitment. Pick a battle you want to win, one you know will make your heart beat faster five days from now, five weeks from now, five months from now... five *years* from now!

You have to be committed to what you do and how you do it. Changing the world is like an addiction: once it's in your veins, you never go back to being the kid you were before. As I was researching this chapter, I was trying to think what I did before *Just Yell Fire*. Before all the meetings and workshops and training sessions and emails and awards, travel and ceremonies, I honestly can't remember; I guess I was wasting a lot of valuable time on kid stuff. It's like I'm a different person now, but it also seems like the revolution was always a part of my life.

I can't remember a time when I wasn't a black belt, when I wasn't speaking to a gathering of high school girls or FBI agents, when I wasn't nervous before a speech or psyched after, wasn't proud to be handing out another FREE *Just Yell Fire* video to a girl whose life it might save, and wasn't up 'til 1 a.m. (sorry, Mom) reading emails from kids just like you who grew angry, became active and started their own revolutions.

It's easy to get excited about fighting injustice, but it's more important to stay committed.

T IS FOR TALENT

9

You HAVE to do what you love. There's just too much work involved, too many late nights and early mornings and missed flights and long, long flights and more to do. So fight injustice but fight the right way; fight *your* way. I would have never had the courage to get up in front of a group of girls to talk about fighting back using the *Just Yell Fire* method if I didn't already love being a black belt and practicing martial arts. Do what you love and you'll do your best work. Do your best work, and people will help you to do it.

In many ways, being a trained street fighter prepared me for creating *Just Yell Fire*; it was like the perfect storm of experience, passion and action that came together to show me the way to my very own personal revolution. *Just Yell Fire* would have been a very different program – or maybe even not a program at all – if I didn't already love martial arts and the feeling of strength and independence it gave me.

I think of all the **Young Revolutionaries Who Rock** that I've met while writing this book and traveling around the world and it's intimidating how much they've done in their chosen fields. Fighting tobacco use and funding cancer research and feeding hungry children and clothing kids who are dirt poor – I often wonder how they do it.

I mean, I know how I do it but how do they do it? I think the answer is the same for all of us: we do what we do because we love it. I feel at home when I'm speaking to a room full of girls or training them in the *Just Yell Fire* techniques. I'm not so sure I could say the same thing if I was touring a homeless shelter or trying to shoot 2,000 hoops or running a marathon for charity.

We each have a comfort zone, a place where we feel comfortable and safe to do our best and most important work. That is where your Revolution should start; that is where you belong.

So what do you love? Maybe you think it's something useless or pointless that could never, ever help a single person – let alone the entire world. Well, you're wrong. Maybe you're into fashion; maybe that's your reason for living. Think that's not important enough to help anybody? Think again!

I know someone who collected prom dresses from all her friends and then from all the girls in her school, and then every school in town, just so girls who can't afford to buy a nice prom dress get to discretely come in and pick one out for free. They actually get to shop for the dress they want, go to the prom feeling like a princess, and they get to experience all the magic of the night just like everyone else.

My friend made this possible. It was hard work, but once you've worn a dress to a prom, you never wear it again, so why not donate it knowing someone will be dancing the night away with their dream date because of you? This is just one of the many examples I know of, personally, where real kids just like you and me made a HUGE difference in the lives of others. It can be recycled prom dresses or anything; just do something!

So never, ever think that what you love won't matter or where you live isn't cool, or that what is important to you isn't important to someone else, or that you're not close enough to a problem to make an impact. Very few **Young Revolutionaries Who Rock** live in thriving metropolises like LA, NY, DC, or ATL. Some live near the tobacco fields of rural North Carolina or in Small Town, America, where there would seem to be little opportunity.

But opportunity doesn't come from where you live; it lives inside of you. Right now I bet you're thinking of something, someone or someplace you could help change but are second-guessing yourself because it's not cool enough, important enough or helpful enough. Just remember, if a revolution can start with CDs, school supplies or a teddy bear – it can sure enough start with you!

11

YOUNG REVOLUTIONARIES WHO ROCK
Vasanth Kuppuswamy, 19

Vasanth with the principal at the
Tamil Nadu School in Volare, India

Did you know that there are kids in this world who can't
go to school because of where they were born? Kids who, if
they *do* get lucky enough to go to school, have to sit on hard
concrete or even dirt floors – all day – with no heat in the
winter or air conditioning in the summer?

Just think about that for a minute the next time you log
onto your in-class computer to do your homework or sign up
for a field trip to somewhere cool or take a hot shower after
gym or chill out in the library where it's always a cool 68
degrees.

It's hard for many of us to believe, but justice is sometimes
blind. And, in some countries – even in our own country – not
every student is created equal. That's why it's so important for
us to fight injustice wherever we find it – even if it's halfway
around the world.

I believe that making a difference is the most important
contribution a person can make. Fortunately, I'm in some
very good company. Our first inductee into the **Young
Revolutionaries Who Rock** Hall of Fame agrees with me. In
fact, making a difference is what college freshman Vasanth

Kuppuswamy is all about. Explains Vasanth, "Any teen can put their mind to something and make a difference."

And he should know. Six years ago Vasanth traveled to distant India to spend the summer in the rural village where his father grew up. With a whole summer to spare and no water parks, movie theaters or Internet cafes to go to, Vasanth did what any young revolutionary would do: he went to the local public school and offered to volunteer his time teaching English to the local students.

The principal was doubtful. He told Vasanth, "No one ever amounted to anything in this village except a servant, shepherd, or a farmhand."

Recalling the experience for an essay he later wrote, Vasanth explained, "Before I even embarked on the journey to teach the students in India that I had volunteered to instruct, I had a long talk with the principal. With a brutal honesty and a defeated spirit, he said that nothing goes into the kids' brains and 'that I was wasting my time.'"

Vasanth explained that the principal's words only motivated him to work harder. "I decided to get involved," he said, "because I knew deep down that the students in the village were capable of being more than just 'servants, shepherds, and farmhands,' to quote the principal. My dad was born in that village and grew up in a poor family yet he was able to make it to America and succeed. If he could do it, why not others?"

Speaking to *Current Events* magazine, Vasanth expressed his dismay with the principal's attitude. "The comments were really surprising because in the United States, we always think that an educator is supposed to be nurturing."

Vasanth had eight weeks to give – and give them he would. What he saw on his first day at the scruffy local school amazed him. The classes – some of them had as many as 60

13

kids in each – sat on the bare concrete floor; there were no desks or chairs. It was summer, dreadfully hot in rural India, yet the school had no air conditioning. Vasanth, who plans to go to medical school, was surprised that there was no science equipment, not even the microscopes and Bunsen burners that American kids take for granted.

Vasanth was undaunted. He had come here to teach. He recalls, "I told the kids that I believed in them. I told them they were destined for better things rather than becoming servants, shepherds, or farmhands. I gave them an extensive speech on how they could accomplish more than what their parents had. They had to believe in themselves as much as I believed in them. The end result was that most of them rose to the occasion."

Vasanth pledged to return the next summer – and the next. He never doubted his intentions, but he realized some of his students and their parents were skeptical. Worse yet, who would teach the children while he was gone? Vasanth remembers, "When I prepared to leave, I had to transfer the keys to their minds back to the principal who would once again become their teacher. Because he had seen the change in the student performances and attitudes as their eyes sparkled with questions while I worked with them, the principal vowed to try harder to inspire these kids and to believe in them."

And so Vasanth returned to South Carolina – and his seventh grade year! While other kids were talking about sunburns and beach trips when their teachers asked "What did YOU do this summer?" Vasanth quietly went about his business – and that business became raising money for the Tamil Nadu School back in India.

Speaking at every Rotary Club, library and community center that would have him, Vasanth told the story of children sitting on concrete floors, no chairs or desks, no heat in the

14

winter or air in the summer, no microscopes or Petri dishes – and the community responded. When Vasanth returned to India that next year, he had $8,000 in his pocket to help refurbish the Tamil Nadu School. Amazingly, the Indian community also responded; the Indian government matched Vasanth's contribution and then some – they contributed an additional $10,000!

He went right to work. Soon the tiny rural town of Tamil Nadu was abuzz with the sound of carpenters sawing and assembling desks and chairs for the students while electricians began installing ceiling fans. They were even able to buy science and math equipment, textbooks and provide uniforms for the students.

And each summer since, Vasanth has worked tirelessly to spread the word about his cause and bring back as much financial support as he can to the students at the Tamil Nadu

15

Vasanth and some of his students in Tamil Nadu, India

School in India. Since his first summer, Vasanth has helped build a wall around the school to keep farm animals off the grounds, added a basketball court and even paid former students' college tuitions (about $250 a year per student in India).

Year after year contributions have increased and, suddenly, it's not just the school benefiting from Vasanth's efforts, but the entire town. Recently Vasanth helped install an expensive water-filtration system for the entire town, all because he saw the injustice facing smart, bright, teachable children who no one else believed in.

Vasanth recalls of his experience, "Now, whenever I reflect on this experience, I realize the significance of having someone believe in you. For those students in that remote area of India, I had become that person, the one who believed in them; the oxygen that fueled their flames. In the process of teaching those students and believing in them, I inspired others such as parents, teachers, and even the principal, but most importantly the students themselves. It is the belief in the students that is the most important factor in education, especially among those kids who lack any believers at all."

The best part is, after so many years being involved with the school, Vasanth is finally starting to see all of his hard work pay off: "There is one boy in the village named Sakthivel. His family lives on less than $1.00 a day. In the eleventh grade, he pretty much had his mind made up to stop school and become a farmer like his dad. I spoke with him in an attempt to talk him out of it and explain that the school was due for dramatic change. I also told him that if he tries a little harder he can go to college and make a name for himself. This past April, he graduated with a Bachelor's Degree in Chemistry and is now looking to get a Master's degree somewhere in Chennai."

Now that's a Revolution worth starting!

16

WHAT YOU CAN DO RIGHT NOW

I'm a pretty lucky girl; I know Vasanth Kuppuswamy personally. In fact, I joined him in India this summer so that I could teach the girls at the Tamil Nadu School as well as 12 colleges throughout Southern India the *Just Yell Fire* program. To listen to Vasanth, you'd never think he'd accomplished all this great stuff; he's really humble and, until you get to know him, pretty shy.

But then he'll start talking about India or his students or his cause and his eyes light up and it's like he's a whole other person standing there. That's what fighting injustice does to you: makes you better, stronger, and just a little bit prouder and louder. Revolutions can be exciting and, like I already warned you, they are downright addictive. Just try stopping someone like Vasanth and you'll see what I mean; it's impossible to stop a revolution once it's started.

17

You don't have to produce a film or travel halfway around the world to start fighting injustice right now. A little while ago I said you should **A.C.T. Now, Think Later**; well, now IS later. So the first thing I want you to do before we move on is to start thinking about the ways you could be of help – locally, nationally or even internationally.

Remember, it doesn't have to be anything expensive, tricky, involved or even that amazing. It doesn't require a passport or a credit card or a bank loan. Just start small and think big; imagine what you could do and, most importantly, what you want to do. Let the pieces come together one by one – the logistics of where and when and why and how it will all happen. For now, begin with the Idea; the rest is details.

Below I've provided space for you to jot down some ideas you may have about the injustices you have encountered, causes you want to pick up or rights you want to fight for. That's right; this is ONE book I encourage you to write in!

Maybe you only write down one thing for now; that's great, fine, super. Bookmark this page and come back to it when inspiration strikes and you've thought of a few more ideas. Keep this book by your bed and if you think of something in the middle of the night, come back here and jot it down.

Or maybe you can think of 10 off the top of your head right now and aren't even reading this anymore! Or, maybe you have more than 10; even better! Go grab some scrap paper and don't stop writing until you're through.

Here goes:

My Personal List of Rights and Fights

1.) _____

2.) _____

3.) _____

4.) _____

5.) _____

6.) _____

7.) _____

8.) _____

9.) _____

10.) _____

Dallas and Vasanth Kuppuswami at the
Caring Awards in Washington, DC

PARTING WORDS ON INJUSTICE

Sadly, injustice is everywhere these days. That's why it's so important for every girl and boy in every neighborhood and in every school to find something to get angry about, get active about, and care enough about to fight for with every ounce of your being!

19

I've seen change happen firsthand. I've talked to girls who learned something from me and I've learned something from them. We're all connected, you and me, us and them, and the only way to make that connection even stronger is to get up, get going and do something about it.

We can all sit at home and complain that the politicians aren't doing enough, that the police aren't protecting us enough, that our teachers don't care enough, but are we any better than they are if we don't get up and do something about it ourselves?

I know it still seems hard because you're a kid, but just look at the great kids I've introduced you to so far. And there are so many more to come. Some of these kids are younger than you and me and they are absolutely rocking change every day of the week. Some of these kids are from broken homes, kids with unbelievably difficult backgrounds or debilitating diseases or other challenges and they're doing twice as much as most of the rest of us.

One person CAN make a difference.

All you have to do is A.C.T.

■

Violins, CDs, DVDs, tire gauges, socks, underwear and even teddy bears. Look at them in a vacuum and they're hardly "weapons of mass inspiration." But look again and you'll see active, dedicated, committed kids just like yourself who have turned these everyday, household items into their own personal ways of fighting injustice and saving the world – one revolution at a time.

■

Dallas with Peyton Manning, Quarterback for
Indianapolis Colts at the Prudential Spirit of
Community Awards in Washington, DC

CHAPTER TWO

I Have the Right
to Live a Life Free of Fear

"No matter how much I give to others, I always receive more in return. Volunteering has changed my perspective about what is really important, and many of the people who mean the most to me now are people who I met through my project. Volunteering is a way of life for me, and I feel privileged to have found my passion so early in life."

—CLAIRE CRAWFORD, Age 18

On my journeys all across this country and speaking with young girls, teenagers and women who've been sexually assaulted, I've heard amazing stories of courage and bravery – not just in their time of extreme danger, facing off with a much stronger, much bigger attacker, but in the quiet, depressing and often lonely aftermath of sexual assault.

These women and girls often endure agonizing months, even years, of painful recovery marked by nightmares, insomnia, depression, fatigue and just plain feeling scared to death all the time.

One thing I've heard over and over again from rape survivors is how they have to literally fight the urge to live what these courageous young girls and women describe as a "fearful life" – where they don't jump at every footstep or freak out at every loud noise; a life where they're not afraid of the dark or to talk to strangers or to get in the car and drive someplace new.

They're so right: fear is a hope killer. It clouds our minds and overloads our circuits, robbing us of our power to think because it overrides our emotions. The biggest challenge I have when presenting *Just Yell Fire* programs is training girls to "fight the fear."

The more they practice their ten get-away moves, the more habitual the moves become because when you're in a panic – when fear overtakes you – it's hard to stop and think about what to do. You can't stop and think; you have to act.

That's how things get done: by doing. Fear puts the brakes on doing and gets you thinking, wondering, and worrying. And that's the challenge young revolutionaries face: it can be scary to face a challenge and overcome it. In the previous chapter you met my friend Vasanth, who brought a poor, outdated Indian school into the 21st century and gave the students a new sense of confidence. They started out with dirt floors and next to no equipment or supplies and now some of them are graduating and going on to college, even getting their Master's Degrees.

I think you'll agree with me that this was a huge challenge to overcome!

In this chapter you'll meet another one of our **Young Revolutionaries Who Rock**, Claire Crawford. Claire was born with a cleft lip and palate, and faced multiple surgeries for most of her sixteen years before the birth defect was finally corrected.

She writes, "I had 9 surgeries—that was only five years without one—and it all started when I was three months old. Not all have been directly for my cleft, but all have been related."

Can you imagine? Being three months old – even three *years* old – and undergoing major facial reconstruction? Claire often felt frightened and anxious during these times, but she knew that the fear wasn't helping, only hurting. She knew she had to find a way to fight the fear – or she'd never get through all the many surgeries she still faced to look "normal."

How did she do it? Claire recalls, "When I was younger, the most important part of undergoing surgery was having a brand new stuffed animal beside me at all times. It was a major crisis if I didn't have it."

Knowing how great a teddy bear made her feel when she was preparing for – and recovering from – surgery, Claire started *"Claire's Bears,"* a non-profit organization that donates free teddy bears to children with cleft palates and those who care for them – doctors, nurses, hospitals, candy stripers, volunteers, and cleft palate researchers.

Claire proudly says, "I began my project, *'Claire's Bears,'* when I was fourteen years old, and I have raised more than $13,000 for 1,300 bears so far." Just think of that: Claire's own little private revolution has not just affected her, but 1,300 kids who might have felt afraid, lonely and desperate without their Claire's Bear by their side as they endure these painful procedures.

25

Don't let fear hold you back from starting your own revolution. Look how easy it is to get started; look how simple it is to change the world – one kid, one teddy bear, and one revolution at a time.

But only if you Fight the Fear.

Being Scared is Temporary; Being Fearful is Forever

Not all fear is created equal. In fact, there is a big difference between **being afraid** and **living in fear**.

Being afraid is a natural emotion. And let's face it: we have plenty to be afraid of. Global warming, rising murder rates, violence every night on the news, danger lurking around every corner, cancer – just about everywhere you turn, there's something else to be afraid about.

But being afraid is a temporary thing. Something happens – a knock at the door late at night, a prank phone call that jolts you out of a deep sleep, missing the bus and being the last one lingering on school property as it gets dark – and you are, temporarily at least, afraid. Your heart races, your adrenaline surges, your palms get moist, the hairs on the back of your neck stand up. But for most of us, the moment quickly resolves itself and the fear passes. The late-night knock at your door turns out to be your neighbor needing to borrow something; the prank phone call turns out to be your little brother's buddies playing a trick on you; your mom shows up with apologies – and an iced coffee to go – to pick you up at school. Problem solved, heart rate back to normal.

26

It's okay to be afraid every once in awhile. Heck, it's perfectly *natural* to be afraid every once in awhile. Fear is a hard-wired reaction to the "fight or flight" response developed by our ancestors, those hale and hearty cavemen and women who had a thousand more reasons to be scared back then than we do now – like saber-tooth tigers and predatory birds the size of a taxi. But it's NOT okay to be fearful a majority of the time. Being fearful is when you're scared of everything – all the time – with no end in sight.

Living in fear is to be scared of just about everything; scared to sit in front of the class because people might shoot spitwads into your hair; scared to raise your hand in history class because you might say something dumb; scared to try out for the school play because you might not get the part; scared to go to a movie alone on a Friday night because, well, someone might see you there alone. This is more than just being afraid of the thing that goes bump in the night; this is being afraid to live your life as it's meant to be lived.

And how can you start a revolution if you're too scared to get out of bed?!?

Look, we can talk all day about what's wrong and what's right, but the main thing you should care about is starting your own revolution – and for some, fear can stop them from doing just that. If you're one of those unfortunate prisoners of fear, I want you to carefully review the next chapter and what I call the **Five Sins of Fear**.

THE FIVE SINS OF FEAR

Why aren't there more revolutions? Why haven't I met 10,000 or 100,000 or 1,000,000 **Young Revolutionaries Who Rock** instead of 100 or 1,000? One simple, spine-tingling reason: **fear**. Fear is what keeps people down when they're being oppressed, what keeps millions of people in line to satisfy the whims of a few chosen leaders, and what keeps us from living the life we're intended to live.

Fear is what keeps us power*less* instead of power*ful*.

Think of how much easier, happier, stronger and even *longer* your life might be *without* fear. Think of how confident you'd be if you weren't afraid to go out in those jeans or that you'd look too chunky in that bikini. Think of how you could rock on the debate team if you weren't so afraid of speaking to crowds, or how you could get into Harvard or Yale if only you weren't afraid that everybody else there would be smarter than you.

Fear doesn't just make us stop thinking; it makes the thoughts that can't get by the "fear barrier" irrational, immature and insincere. We know we're smart, strong, young, powerful, beautiful and energetic, yet fear causes us to doubt those very traits that make us so special in the first place.

Well, it doesn't have to be that way. I'm going to share with you The **5 Sins of Fear** so you can spot them when they

27

pop up – and slam them down whenever they show their ugly faces when you're trying to enjoy a day at the beach, a night at the movies (with or without your friends) or your own private revolution.

That way you can live with less fear in your life – and more revolutions:

1.) **Fear makes you doubt yourself:** When you are afraid, you feel powerless. When you feel powerless, you doubt yourself – your abilities, your strength, even your character. No matter how good our intentions may be, no matter what revolution we may be plotting, we're not going to get very far if doubt creeps up every few minutes. Inspiration is a big part of changing the world, but doubt is one fear that is a big inspiration-killer.

28

2.) **Fear makes you trust others too much:** Don't get me wrong – part of being human means trusting other people. Even young revolutionaries need mentors, teachers, counselors and experts to help keep the revolution going. But trust is earned, not simply given. When you live in fear, you look to others for help too often. And the more you seek help from others, the less likely you are to look where it counts the most: inside yourself.

3.) **Fear holds you back:** Fear doesn't just stop you from moving forward, it stops you dead in your tracks. You... and all your ambitions, hopes and dreams. Fear holds you back from your agenda because you're afraid you might fail, look stupid or even be sent home. Who knows what we could accomplish if we weren't so afraid all the time? Get rid of fear... and find out!

4.) **Fear limits you to a half life:** When you are fearful, you are only living a half life. Think about it: we swim out only so far in the ocean because we're afraid of what lurks just past that last wave. We ride our bikes only so far along the trail because we're afraid we might get a flat and have to walk all the way home. But how far could you go if you just swam a little farther or rode a little longer? You'll never know if fear guides your life because fear only lets you live half a life.

5.) **Fear is addictive:** Probably the worst thing about fear is that it is addictive; it sucks you in until you're so used to fear that you just don't know anything else. Researchers estimate that the average person has about 50,000 thoughts a day. Unfortunately, researchers also believe that a majority of those thoughts are negative, even fearful. We have got to start replacing some, if not all, of our fearful thoughts with positive ones. Switch out your addiction to fear with an addiction to positivity, hope and possibility.

29

Remember, a true hero isn't somebody who feels NO fear. A true hero is someone who does the right thing even though they are afraid to do it. They do it because it is the right thing to do. If it is easy and you already know how to do it, if you know what the outcome will be – and there is absolutely no risk – then there is also absolutely no courage involved.

Fear is normal. Fear is a good thing to have; it can save you, protect you, warn you, and help you, but you have to be able to figure out what kind of fear it is. If it is just a fear of the unknown, then keep going, find your courage and tread lightly, but never stop. That's what makes a true hero.

YOUNG REVOLUTIONARIES WHO ROCK

Claire Crawford, 18

Claire Crawford with Cleft patient

Claire Crawford knows a thing or two about fear. Claire was born with a cleft lip and palate, a facial deformity which greatly impairs the speech, hearing, speaking, breathing and eating abilities of the affected person if it is not surgically corrected. The deformity occurs during fetal growth and leaves a gap between the nose and lip as well as in the roof of the mouth.

30

To correct her deformity, Claire has had multiple surgeries; one for almost every year she's been alive. As she says, "At three months old, I had my first corrective surgery." We all know what it's like to go to the doctor's office when we were kids, but imagine getting major surgery in your infancy.

Claire remembers how fearful she used to be during those surgeries: "I remember feeling anxiety, fear, and being so apprehensive! It frightened me to have tests before surgery, to have blood taken, and then to have to put on a hospital gown... I knew what all that meant! As I got older, the anticipation for months prior to the procedure eventually led to a type of morning anxiety during late spring, the time of year when most of my surgeries took place."

Most of us think of spring as a time of fun and rebirth; spring break and chocolate Easter bunnies and time to get out of the house after a long, dull winter – but not for Claire. Can you imagine dreading the spring because you knew each time the snow melted or the lilies bloomed, you'd have to endure another long operation and slow, painful recovery?

Many times Claire found herself lonely and isolated in a hospital room, but thankfully her parents were never too far away and everyone was always supportive of her efforts to correct her deformity and live a healthy, happy life.

It all paid off. Explains Claire, "Now, seventeen years and nine surgeries later, I have completed all surgical and dental work on my cleft, and I am healthy and happy." But Claire never forgot the doctors who helped her, the nurses who cared for her, the fellow patients who kept her company, or even those kids who still have cleft lips and palates to contend with and many, many surgeries to endure.

31

Claire wanted to give back to other kids with cranial-facial defects, and she soon realized how she could start her own personal healthcare revolution. "I have always liked having stuffed animals and toys around, but having a stuffed animal in surgery has been particularly important," says Claire. "I remember one gift given to me that stood out when I was preparing for surgery: a plain, simple brown bear given to me by the hospital where the procedures were to take place. In that bear I saw a friend and companion that would endure any pain that I felt or any fear that I suffered. It was something to hold, take care of, and love."

In the same way that little stuffed bear meant so much to Claire, she knew she could help others by handing bears out to other children with cleft palates heading for surgery. And so *Claire's Bears* was born.

Explains Claire: "I've been collecting donations from my community, friends and family to purchase some cleft teddy bears from the Cleft Palate Foundation to give to a childrens' hospital in Jackson, MS, cleft palate teams, and to individuals I know who have a cleft lip/palate. The cleft teddy bears have a tag that includes resources for finding out more about clefts, including the Cleftline telephone number and website with information and resources, along with stories like this one, that give hope to parents, children, and teenagers."

Since then, Claire figures she's handed out hundreds of the teddy bears to kids in need; hundreds more have been sent around the nation – and around the world. Claire started her revolution the only way she knew how: by giving what she could to those with whom she had a common bond. It wasn't fancy or technological or even very adult, for that matter. It was just a simple teddy bear; something only a child could love – designed just for kids.

Make that *very special kids*. "I really wanted to provide other cleft-affected children with the same amount of comfort and love that I had when I was growing up. I knew how difficult it was socially and mentally to undergo so many surgeries and to have a visible scar which provokes constant questions that make you so self-conscious of your appearance. The cleft child's speech impediment often creates a shy personality and unwillingness to speak to others, so I wanted to help these children build up their confidence. Also, I knew that most adults don't know what a cleft lip and palate is, even though it's the fourth most common birth defect in the world, so I wanted to raise awareness about the deformity and teach others how to respond with kind understanding when meeting a person with a cleft."

The best part is Claire started with a very small base of time, money and effort. "When I was fourteen years old," she recalls, "I did some research and realized for the first time how many other children had a cleft lip and palate. I noticed that many children didn't have the great amount of support I had while I was growing up and having surgeries, and I knew that children in developing countries often go without necessary surgeries because they can't afford them.

"I found a website for the Cleft Palate Foundation which provides information for cleft patients and their parents and sells 'cleft teddy bears,' which have stitches above their lips as cleft children do after their first surgeries. I also saw the Operation Smile website, which sends volunteers to developing countries to operate on cleft children. After finding these volunteer organizations which are focused on helping cleft children like me, I knew that I could get involved, too."

How did Claire get started? Did she have to go to a ton of trouble, raise a lot of money or ask a lot of adults for help? As Claire tells it, none of the above: "The first step I took in my project was ordering a cleft teddy bear for me. Once I received it, I remembered the many times a stuffed animal had brought me comfort during surgeries. I decided to ask my community to help me provide the special bears for other cleft children, and I received an amazing response.

"I set an original goal of 25 bears for $250, but within a month I had donations for more than ten times that amount. I also volunteered to share my story as a cleft patient with medical and volunteer groups in my community, and after speaking to several local groups I was invited to statewide and national groups as an inspirational speaker. This became another form of fundraising because – even though I never ask for donations during presentations – many people realize that it only takes $10 to change a child's life with a teddy bear."

33

And did she ever: $13,000 and 1,300 teddy bears later, Claire – and *Claire's Bears* – are still going strong. She has helped so many people, all their stories could fill a book. But when I asked her, Claire was eager to share one very special story of how *Claire's Bears* helped touch a child just like her:

"Throughout the three years that I have been a volunteer," Claire remembers, "I have encountered countless individuals who have changed my life more than I could change theirs. One particular child was a boy I met during an Operation Smile medical mission to the Philippines. I was a student volunteer on the mission trip, and I accompanied 50 medical volunteers and another student. I talked to and entertained cleft children before their surgeries. One activity that the children really enjoyed was blowing bubbles, and while I was playing with a group I noticed a shy boy standing in the corner and watching us. I tried to get him to join us, and when he wouldn't I blew bubbles toward him. He immediately started smiling and laughing, encouraging me to continue. I looked over at his mother sitting across the room, and she was beaming—she wasn't used to seeing anyone play with her child because he looked different.

"The next day I checked the list of children who were scheduled for surgery, and there was his name: Austin Aleo. I rejoiced with his family, who had traveled for days in hopes that little Austin would have a chance at a normal life. Before his surgery the next day, I handed him one of the cleft teddy bears I had brought from home, and I showed him the stitches on the bear's lip and the scar on my lip.

"He stroked the stitches and held his bear tightly as he was put to sleep on the operating table. When I saw him in the post-operation room hours later, his lip was beautifully stitched together and he was smiling slightly as he slept. When he and his family left, his mother handed me her earrings, the only jewelry she had, and a card telling how much she appreciated my student partner and I treating her son like a brother. She said she would never forget our kindness. I will never forget her smile."

And here is probably the greatest reason for starting your own personal revolution. Don't do it for fame, for money, or to

Dallas with Claire Crawford

35

go on all those upscale trips I described in my introduction to this book; do it for one person at a time and your life will be full of stories like Claire's, like Austin's, like Vasanth's, and all the other **Young Revolutionaries Who Rock**. In the end, revolutions aren't about instant gratification or popularity polls or bank accounts or Doritos bags or plaques on the wall; they're about people in need and those who help.

What advice does Claire have for the rest of us?

"As long as you are following your passion," she explains, "you will achieve the goals you set and many more. Even if the process seems long and sometimes impossible, take it one step at a time and be prepared to defend your beliefs. Some people will say that one person – especially a teenager – cannot change the world, but the truth is any person can effect change. All it takes is passion in your heart and the willingness to, as Ghandi said, 'Be the change you wish to see in the world.' Also, remember that in the world you may be one person, but to one person you may be the world."

I think you'll agree with me, that's great advice indeed!

WHAT ARE YOU SO AFRAID OF?

As you can see, Claire faced her fears to start her own personal revolution. It wasn't easy, but I think the greatest thing about these young revolutionaries we've met so far – Vasanth and Claire – is that they didn't let fear or barriers or obstacles or insecurity stop them from impacting the lives of others.

We all have good intentions. I think my family must have shelled out a thousand dollars last year just because every time I pick up the phone and somebody asks for money –the Make-a-Wish Foundation, the Cancer Cure Fund – I always pledge as much as we can.

But giving money is only part of the solution. You could pour money into Red Cross and the Salvation Army, as much as you could afford, and it would still be only a drop in the bucket. That doesn't mean you don't give what you can, but as kids… how much can we really give? How can we make a big impact?

That's why acting on your good intentions by starting your own revolution is the best solution for kids like us. That way, all it costs is our time and we can personalize it to fight for the rights, the causes and the charities we believe in.

Claire believed the best place she could wade in and help was the place where she felt most comfortable: amongst kids just like her. Now, I get freaked out if my face breaks out before a school day, big function or spring dance; I can't imagine going through endless surgeries just to fit in and look like everyone else, but to hear Claire tell it, it was all part of the plan. And even when she achieved her goal, she didn't stop there. *Claire's Bears* is still going strong, still raising funds, still giving out teddy bears, and I know for sure that the next time I talk to Claire, she's going to have another story about another little boy or girl that will bring us both to tears of joy.

That's the greatest thing about starting a revolution: you get as much as you give, usually a whole lot more.

But I know what you're thinking: "Vasanth and Claire are special people; it's easy for *them* to start a Revolution." I agree; they are special people. But so are you. Even though I've never met you I know you're special because here you are reading this book instead of gabbing with your friends, texting, watching TV or surfing the Internet. And you're wrong about one more thing: it *wasn't* all that easy for Vasanth and Claire to start a revolution – but they did it anyway.

How? They succeeded by overcoming their fears, by saying "no" to their doubts and insecurities and, in Vasanth's case, saying "no" to the principal who told him his students would never amount to more than farmers and shepherds. Claire and Vasanth fought back and they fought hard, but their biggest victory was against their very own fears, doubts and insecurities.

And now it's time for you to do the same thing. But first you'll need to identify your fears in order to overcome them. So use the handy form below to list everything you're afraid of, and then in the last few sections I'll tell you how each and every fear can be overcome:

Things I'm Afraid Of

_____   _____

_____   _____

_____   _____

_____   _____

_____   _____

_____   _____

_____   _____

_____   _____

_____   _____

_____   _____

_____   _____

_____   _____

How to Live a Fearless Life:
3 Questions for the Fearful Revolutionary

How can you live a fearless life? I'm glad you asked, because the sooner you stop being afraid – afraid of crowds, afraid of public speaking, afraid of asking for help, time or money – the sooner your own personal revolution can start. Now, don't get me wrong; I'm not saying that I'm never afraid – I am – or that you should strive to never be afraid. Being afraid is one of nature's gifts to help us be alert and aware of our surroundings.

Without fear we'd be careless, take too many risks and put ourselves in harm's way by not being alerted to the very real and constant dangers that exist in our modern world. In fact, part of my *Just Yell Fire* safety training program is about heeding your fears, taking them seriously and responding to them appropriately. So I'm not saying "never fear" or suggesting that you should be entirely fearless. No, what I'm saying is that we need to put fear into perspective and treat it like an exception and not an everyday thing.

Some people really do feel fearful all day, every day. And not just the ones in mental hospitals or psychiatrists' offices, but regular, everyday people like you and me. From the moment they get up they're afraid they've done something wrong, that someone will blame them for something they didn't do, or catch them doing something they shouldn't, or ridicule, criticize or bully them for no good reason.

When they're driving to school or work they're afraid of the cars behind them, next to them and in front of them. When they get where they're going, they're afraid there won't be a good parking space or that they'll leave their lights on and the car won't start. When they go to the movies they're afraid all the good seats will be taken or the popcorn will

39

run out or the projector will break. When they get ready to go to bed at night, they're afraid they didn't lock the front door or that there won't be enough OJ or milk for breakfast the next morning. In short, if they don't have something to worry about, they'll create something.

My mom calls it "borrowing trouble," and I think that phrase fits so perfectly when we talk about creating our own fearful life. It's like when everything is going well we say to ourselves, "Hmmm, nothing bad's going on, life is great, I'm absolutely, 100% perfectly fine, not a trouble in the world. Here, let me go borrow a problem so I have something to feel bad about!"

And that's the thing about fear: so much of it is self-created. We think our lives are going too well, we think we've got it too good, we think, "No way can this last forever; something bad is going to happen – and soon!" We're sure things can't last and something bad will happen, so what do we do? We make sure something bad happens by filling our lives with fear. We find things to be afraid of, more and more often, until we're blinded, hooked and literally **addicted to fear**.

Fear has a way of making us believe things that aren't true. I mean, do we really think the popcorn's going to run out at the movie theater or that we didn't lock the door before bed, even though we've already checked it five times? By getting into the habit of seeing things clearly, realistically, and logically, instead of viewing them fearfully and irrationally, you can conquer fear one anxiety attack at a time.

So the next time you start to feel fearful, the next time you feel that flutter in your stomach and you get anxious all over again, ask yourself these three questions and you will soon get into the habit of being less fearful:

40

1.) **"Am I really in danger?"** Fear is a human response designed to alert us to danger – real, physical danger – and yet so often we feel fear even when there *is* no present danger. Fear of bad grades, of pimples, of a potential date turning you down or an acquaintance asking you out – are these things really *dangerous?* So when you start to feel fearful, ask yourself if you're really in danger. If so, react accordingly. Lock the door, run, or *Just Yell Fire!* If not, realize that your fear is probably not well-grounded and try to replace it with something more positive – like maybe a good laugh at how silly it was to be afraid in the first place.

2.) **"Is what I'm afraid of really *that* bad?"** A lot of our fears are self-created; we invent them where they don't really exist. Focus on one thing for too long – that big test on Friday, that zit on your forehead, that hot guy in homeroom – and you're bound to conjure up all kinds of dark and scary possibilities after awhile. Maybe it's because we have too much time on our hands and our brain has nothing more constructive to think about. Whatever the case, think about the outcome of what scares you. Then ask yourself, "Is it really that bad, after all?" How about that test on Friday? Will it make or break my GPA? And is that zit really that big? And didn't I just buy that awesome cover-up at the mall? And is that guy in homeroom really that hot? And so what if he is? Either he'll make a move or he won't. Maybe I'll make a move this time. Either way, I can deal with any situation appropriately without resorting to fear.

3.) **"What's the worst that could happen?"** I always consider the worst-case scenario when I'm afraid

41

because, usually, "worst case" really isn't that bad after all. Let's say you get fearful in crowded places and your best friend just asked you to a big concert on Friday night. You really want to go, you know you'll have fun once you get there, but all of a sudden you are overwhelmed by a long list of irrational fears: **a.**) A big fire might break out **b.**) You might have to go to the bathroom in the middle of the concert **c.**) The power might go out and you'll be stuck in the middle of 10,000 screaming fans! Well, think about it for a minute. What are the odds of a fire breaking out at a concert? Pretty small, huh? And if you're that worried about it, agree to go BUT get your friend to agree to hang out near an exit and watch the show from there. And what if you *do* have to go to the bathroom? So what? So you miss a few minutes of the show. And if the power goes out? Well, you're already standing near the exit anyway. You'll have a nice bright "Exit" sign right over your head to show you the way out! So you see, in this case, worst case scenario isn't so bad after all.

42

PARTING WORDS ON FEAR

Now that this chapter is almost over, I want you to close the door on something else, too: FEAR. Life can be great without fear; now go out there and start living fearlessly! I know it won't be easy at first, especially if you're one of those fearful people I've been talking about for the last ten pages or so.

But I've given you the tools to deal with fear, and the best part is that they actually work if you apply them to your daily life. And I do mean daily. Just as fear is addictive, so too is fearlessness! The less fear you feel tomorrow, the less fear you'll feel the day after that, and the day after that.

We also know the opposite to be true: the more fear you feel today, the more fear you'll feel tomorrow and the day after that and the day after that. So the choice is yours to make: to live with fear or without fear.

The great thing is the choice really IS up to you. Yes, when a bear attacks you should get scared. Sure, when you're stuck in a downpour and have to pull to the side of the road before you can drive again, you should be a little anxious until the rain lets up and visibility improves. And, okay, when the principal calls your name over the intercom to ask you to come to his office, that is probably the right time to freak out *just* a bit.

But since fear is an emotional response, we can counter that one-two "fear punch" by thinking rationally about our fears, not emotionally. For instance, did you know that you're more likely to get struck by lightning than you to get attacked by a bear? And if you're scared of driving in the rain, check the weather channel before you grab your car keys. A simple viewing choice could just keep you out of harm's way before you even get on the road. And who knows why the principal is calling you into his office? Maybe it's because you just won some award or honor, and not because he wants to expel you for the rest of the year!

So your biggest ally in the war against fear isn't a gun or a knife, but your brain. Think, think and then think some more about the root cause of your fear, and I'm sure you'll stop being afraid and realize just how much time you've lost to being fearful in the past.

Promise yourself that every time you get scared from now on you will analyze that fear and, if it was unfounded – which I'm betting it's going to be 99 times out of 100 – that you'll do something positive for yourself instead of being afraid. Go for a jog, text a friend, see a movie, read a book, blast your iPod or just plain laugh at yourself for being such a scaredy-cat in the first place.

Whatever you do, the less afraid you feel, the less afraid you'll be.

And fearless kids make GREAT revolutionaries!

44

People magazine photo shoot

■

Researchers estimate that the average human being has about 50,000 thoughts a day. Unfortunately, researchers also believe that a majority of those thoughts are negative, even fearful. We have got to start replacing some, if not all, of our fearful thoughts with more positive ones. Switch out your addiction to fear with an addiction to positivity, hope and possibility.

■

Dallas and Park Maguire on the set
of *Good Morning America*

CHAPTER THREE
I Have the Right
to Believe in Myself

"Meeting with my elected officials has helped me to become a better informed advocate, ultimately resulting in more changes in my community."

—CHAD BULLOCK, Age 20

If there's one thing I know about kids, it's that we don't like to be unpopular – not for a day, not for an hour, not for a minute, not for one hot second. In fact, we'll go to great lengths *not* to offend or insult anyone, if only to make everybody happy so that nobody thinks we're weird or strange.

But what if you believed in something so strongly – believed in *yourself* so strongly – that you were willing to go against what was popular, even against your friends, your family or a major corporation, in order to do what you thought was right?

That's what happened when young revolutionary Chad Bullock took on the Williamson Tobacco Company's 2004 "Kool Mix" launch campaign, which marketed their Kool brand cigarettes using hip-hop music and urban images to sell cigarettes.

Chad was a senior at Middle College High School when he noticed the Kool Mix marketing campaign was targeting mostly urban stores in predominantly black neighborhoods.

Now, most of us would see the ads, frown, shake our heads and walk on by or ignore them altogether. It's the cigarette companies, right? What can one measly kid do about *them*? Nothing, right?

But not this young revolutionary. He and a few of his friends secretly taped the ad campaigns in action at urban neighborhood convenience stores and then sent them to their local Attorney General. In no time, Williamson Tobacco had settled the case and the ads were pulled.

"We drafted a letter to Attorney General Roy Cooper," Chad recently told WRAL-TV in Durham, "and after we sent the letter, he got some of his attorney general friends and they eventually got together and drafted the lawsuit against the tobacco company and it was settled." Just like that, one young revolutionary had single-handedly changed the way a major tobacco company marketed their products to urban youth. Who knows how many kids turned away from smoking because Chad Bullock believed in himself enough to take a stand against the big tobacco companies – and won!

You'll hear more about Chad later on in this chapter, but I just wanted to share his amazing story with you now because it's such a shining example of what we can do – if only we believe in ourselves.

THE SELF-BELIEF QUIZ

How much do you believe in yourself? I mean really, really believe in yourself? You might think the answer is "a lot" or "very much" or even "absolutely 100%," but you might be surprised by how much easier it is to doubt yourself than believe in yourself.

Don't believe me? Read the following statements, and then circle "True" or "False" depending on how much you believe the statement is accurate:

1.) I believe I could compete in the Olympics if I really wanted to.
    a.) True
    b.) False

2.) I believe I could be president of the United States one day if I really wanted to.
    a.) True
    b.) False

3.) I believe I could be Homecoming King/Queen if I really wanted to.
    a.) True
    b.) False

So, how'd you do, you Olympic gold medalist, future president and Homecoming King/Queen? What's that you say? You mean you don't believe you could compete in the Olympics, be elected president, or be crowned on Homecoming? But I thought you said you believed in yourself?

The truth is we're much more likely to doubt ourselves than we are to believe in ourselves. Part of that is because of the society we live in: we're taught that we have to start training at five- or six years old to make it to the Olympics; that only lawyers, senators and congressmen can be elected president; and that only the beautiful, popular people are crowned on Homecoming. And no matter how pretty or popular we may be, we always seem to think we're not quite as pretty or popular – or smart or handsome or athletic or talented – as other people tend to think we are.

Part of it is that we run ourselves down constantly. Listen to your friends the next time you hang out: a lot of

49

conversation will be spent in the negative sphere where you'll hear comments like, "I just wish I could lose these last ten pounds," or "If only I would have studied more for that test," or even "I wish I wasn't so stupid!"

We have to turn the tide in how we think, talk and believe in ourselves if we're really going to be **Young Revolutionaries Who Rock**. The best part about this whole process is that believing in ourselves starts from within and not with what others think of us.

SELF-BELIEF IS A HABIT, NOT A GIFT

Why is it so important to believe in yourself? Simple: when you believe in yourself, you are able to do more, live more, act more and be more. Think of how much more you could accomplish if you weren't always doubting yourself, questioning your instincts or second-guessing your actions. Not that doubt is all bad; we need a healthy dose of self-doubt so that our egos don't get as big as our heads!

But the big question becomes how much doubt is *too* much doubt?

Self-belief means that you acknowledge the doubt, analyze it… but do the right thing anyway. Let's say you want to run for class president because you have some really good ideas about how your school can change for the better. Now, that's a great reason to run for office and the very fact that you're thinking along those lines means that you're already pre-qualified to start your campaign. But what else does it take to be student body prez?

Well, I would think that attending regular meetings before, during and after school would mean you'd have to be pretty darned disciplined. You'd also be leading several other people – vice president, treasurer, secretary – so you need to play well with others. You'd probably have to be organized, considering all the great ideas you have for changing the school and how each one would probably have a file or at least a little paperwork, facts and figures to back up your ideas. And, finally, I think you'd have to be fairly patient because not everything you want to get done is going to happen when you want it to happen – if ever.

So, let's see: **1.**) Disciplined **2.**) Plays well with others **3.**) Organized **4.**) Patient. Are you all those things? If you are, then what's stopping you from running for office? Oh, that's right: you don't believe you can really do it. Or, if you believe you CAN run, you don't believe you can WIN the election.

And THAT is why it's so important to believe in yourself; when you don't, it stops you from doing those things you know you can do, should do and really want to do, but don't do because fear, insecurity and self-doubt stop you from moving forward.

Not believing in yourself costs you valuable progress every single day. It makes you hesitate before you act. It makes you walk past the "Auditions" poster for the new school play because you don't believe you're good enough to get the part the same way it makes you walk straight past the gym after school even though you know it's the big day for cheerleader try-outs.

Worst of all, you can't start a revolution out there – in the world – if you can't look deep inside and believe that you've got the right stuff to be a young revolutionary in the first place. But here's a little secret: every one of these **Young Revolutionaries Who Rock** told me they felt doubt… **but did the right thing anyway**. We are not immune to doubt; far from it. We simply took a booster shot of self-confidence and went out in the world and started our revolutions anyway.

Now it's your turn!

51

3 STEPS TO BELIEVING IN YOURSELF

If you're training to run a marathon, you don't just get up the morning of the race and lace up your brand new Nikes and expect to get to the finish line in one piece. No, you start weeks, even months earlier by running one mile at a time, then two, and then three, until eventually you're running a dozen or more miles per day and inching your body toward the finish line before you even start the race. Training and persistence are to a marathon what planning and organization are to a revolution; you need both if you're ever going to reach your goal.

Believing in yourself is a lot like a marathon; if it's going to last forever, you need to start training today. But how do you "train" to believe in yourself? Well, the first place you start is by realizing that a strong belief in yourself doesn't just happen – like anything else that's worthwhile in life, you're going to have to *make* it happen.

These three steps can help you develop confidence in yourself:

> 1.) **MAKE THE LIST:** I don't often use ALL CAPS because, let's face it, it's REALLY ANNOYING. But this is one time where they actually work in our favor. THE LIST is all the things **you believe yourself to be**. Everything, all of it, goes on THE LIST: Funny. A good athlete. Generous. A great friend. Kind. A smart student. Prompt. Friendly, etc. Take as long as you like. Use scratch paper, use a blank sheet of notebook paper – use a whole legal pad or spiral-bound notebook, whatever it takes. The important thing is to write down every good quality you have; every single one. Don't make them up; don't write them down if they're not true. I mean, if you're actually stingy, don't write down "generous." If you're kind of a

jerk, don't write down "kind." The only way to believe in you more strongly is to see the evidence in black and white. THE LIST is evidence that you should believe in yourself because, well, look at all the ways you're great, wonderful and super.

2.) Circle Your Top 10 Qualities: Now, all that raw data from THE LIST needs to be tightened up and narrowed down so you can focus on – and believe in – your very best qualities. So go through THE LIST and circle your Top 10 Qualities. Okay, I can be flexible here: if it's a really *long* list, make it your Top 20 Qualities; if it's a short list, make it your Top 5. The point here isn't to be so strict or rigid that the rules ruin the point of the exercise, but to pick out those qualities you most admire about yourself – your strength, your compassion, your courage, your thoughtfulness – and hone in on them as you prepare for the next step toward declaring your very own revolution.

53

3.) Act on 1 Quality per Day: Remember: habits are created, not given. So when you do small things every day, they slowly become integrated into your behavior and that's how habits are born. This rule applies to all habits: the good, the bad and the ugly. So now that you've made THE LIST and narrowed it down to your Top 10 Qualities, pick one quality per day and *act on it*. Let's say one of your favorite qualities on THE LIST is Generosity. If so, be generous all day for one entire day. Open the door for others, give up your cab to the person waiting impatiently behind you, let the girl with one item go ahead of you at the cash register, and do the dishes even though it's your little brother's night.

Then, the next day, pick another quality to expand upon; maybe it's Promptness. So, all that day, get everywhere on time: don't be late for class, for work, for practice, for that babysitting job, for your big date. When you get to the end of your list, start again at the top and repeat the process until you have completely integrated all 5, 10, 15 or 20 of those great qualities into permanent habits! The more you do every day to keep these qualities in play, the stronger the habit will become for you – and the sooner you'll believe and recognize that you really are generous, prompt and all those other wonderful things you wrote about yourself on THE LIST.

YOUNG REVOLUTIONARIES WHO ROCK
Chad Bullock, 20

Chad Bullock lives smack dab in the middle of tobacco country: Durham, North Carolina. In fact, according to the North Carolina Department of Agriculture and Consumer Services, "The Tarheel State continues to rank number one in the production of tobacco with an approximate 2007 annual farm income of $587 million."

So Chad was front and center for what would later become the driving principle of his young life. Explains Chad: "Living in North Carolina, a tobacco state, I am surrounded by tobacco warehouses, near tobacco farmers and tobacco company employees. I also see so many of my peers using tobacco and they are not informed about what they are doing to themselves."

Now, we all know how bad tobacco, nicotine and smoking in general can be for our health. According to the American Cancer Society®, "Lung cancer is the second most common cancer in both men and women. It accounts for about 15% of all new cancers. During 2008, there will be about 215,020 new cases of lung cancer."

55

Chad doesn't need statistics to tell him how dangerous smoking can be; he sees it every day when he comes home from school. Chad says, "My grandmother smokes and my grandfather died of lung cancer."

Like most of us, Chad knows the deadly statistics. Unlike most of us, however, he wasn't content with shrugging his shoulders and moving on. Such was Chad's conviction that older people should quit smoking and that younger people should never start that he decided to do something about it.

Chad's two main goals are to inform the general public – and specifically, kids – about tobacco use among youth, as well as reveal deceptive tobacco industry tactics. "I want to reduce the number of teens who pick up this deadly habit," he explains. "I also want to hold the tobacco industry accountable for what they are doing to the health of our world."

So why did Chad get involved in the first place? "I got involved because it was a chance to better my community while bettering myself," explains the young revolutionary. "Seeing almost half a million people DIE each year from a preventable death is wrong."

Chad – who has met Hillary Clinton and Barack Obama through his anti-tobacco work – didn't wait until he was through with college, working for the government, or into adulthood to get started saving lives; he started right where he was. "I asked at school if there was anything I could do to get involved," says Chad. "There are tons of things to do; we just need to seek them out."

And did he ever! Not only was Chad instrumental in shutting down Williamson Tobacco Company's 2004 "Kool Mix" marketing campaign, but he's also turned his attention toward making public places "smoke free" settings where non-smokers can eat or relax in peace and where smokers can be encouraged to quit.

According to *DoSomething.org*, "Durham Bulls Athletic Park allowed cigarette smoking. Deadly secondhand smoke was everywhere, from the seating area to the children's play area; smoke consumed the air. Chad Bullock and his peers have taken action to get this unhealthy issue resolved. Chad and his group have met with the management team and gathered community support through fan surveys. In early 2007, the Durham Bulls announced that they are making the park smoke-free immediately."

All it took for a stadium to change its errant ways was one young revolutionary to speak up, ask other fans to join him, and present their position to management. Think how many other stadiums, restaurants, theaters and other smoking venues could be smoke free – right now – if only more young revolutionaries believed in themselves strongly enough to take a stand and act on those beliefs. Chad has also spoken with the CEO of the Golden Corral restaurants – whose corporate offices are in Raleigh – to make the growing food chain yet another smoke-free environment in North Carolina and beyond.

57

Corporation by corporation, public place by public place and person by person, Chad's passion to help others centers on his belief that not only is smoking deadly, but just plain wrong. It takes a lot of courage to face down corporate chieftains and head honchos at places like stadiums and restaurant chains, let alone major tobacco companies; it takes even more conviction to get them to change corporate policy that may negatively effect their bottom line profits. But most of all, what it takes to do what Chad's done is **a very strong sense of belief in yourself**.

The beauty of Chad's revolution is that his tireless, selfless efforts help others believe in themselves as well. "When I see youth all over the country say that they are ready to go out and make changes, I get really inspired and excited to do more. There was one girl who quit smoking because of something I posted on *facebook.com* about tobacco and that was really inspiring," Chad says.

So, what advice does Chad have for other young revolutionaries? "Don't set barriers or limits. You do not need a lot to make a lot of change. Also, don't be afraid to question authority and let your thoughts be heard."

Chad was one of the other nominees in my category for the *Teen Choice Awards,* and he won. For his efforts and his cause, he picked up $100,000 to keep going.

That is what believing in yourself can do.

Dallas and Chad at the *Teen Choice Awards*

THE FOUR GIFTS OF SELF-BELIEF

You, too, can believe in yourself and start a revolution of your own. It won't be easy at first, but the more you believe in yourself, the easier it will get. Just ask Chad Bullock! But Chad can't help you believe in yourself – and I can't help you either – if you don't start with the one person who really counts most: you.

So maybe you need a little incentive to believe in yourself. Maybe, like most of us, you're asking yourself right about now, "Okay, sure, but what's in it for *me*?" Well, you're in luck because the **Four Gifts of Self-Belief** should have you taking stock in yourself in no time:

1.) **Peace:** When was the last time you truly felt at peace in your own skin? Like everything was right in the world because you finally felt right with yourself? I admit it doesn't happen very often. Most of the time we're so upset, flustered, fearful or angry that peace is the last thing on our minds. But the more peaceful you feel, the happier and more content you are. And the path to this sort of peace starts with believing in yourself, your abilities, your strengths, your habits and your personality.

2.) **Confidence:** We've already talked about how confidence is the birthplace of revolution, but there's no way to have confidence – *true* confidence – if you don't believe in yourself first. Oh, sure, you can tell yourself you're confident, even fake it, but if you don't really *believe* your revolution can succeed, it's just not going to happen. (No matter how badly you want it to).

59

3.) **Trust:** There are very few things in this world we can trust. Some politicians lie, your favorite celebrity can be scandal-ridden, even your parents, mentors, teachers and clergy can disappoint you by making mistakes. But there must be one person in this world you trust above all others – and that person is you. When you believe in yourself, you start to trust yourself more and more. And when you trust yourself, *anything* is possible.

4.) **Energy:** One of the greatest gifts that comes from believing in yourself is the energy you feel that enables you to do almost anything you set your mind to. When you truly believe that you can do just about anything, trust me, you WILL want to go out and get things done. Energy is addictive; the more you feel it, the more you want it, and the more you cultivate it. I can't tell you how great it feels to wake up every morning and jump out of bed knowing you're going to do something special for the world and believing in yourself to the point that you can keep on doing it forever. I can tell you about it, but if you want to know what it feels like, you're going to have to go out there and find out for yourself. All it takes is for one person to believe in you and, of course, that one person... is YOU!

■

If you're training to run a marathon, you don't just get up the morning of the race and lace up your brand new Nikes. No, you start weeks, even months earlier by running one mile at a time, then two, and then three, until eventually you're running a dozen or more miles per day and inching your body toward the finish line before you even start the race. Believing in yourself is a lot like running a marathon; for your revolution to succeed, you need to start training today.

■

Seventeen magazine office NY, NY

Part Two
GET ACTIVE

Dallas filming a music video with
rock sensation Enation

CHAPTER FOUR
I Have the Right
to Fix What's Broken

"Always follow your heart and never give up in hard situations."

—ANA DODSON, Age 16

Peru might seem like it's a world away from me and you, but if there's one thing I've learned from my somewhat nomadic existence it's that kids are the same no matter where you go. After another summer abroad I can tell you that teenagers will be teenagers – be it in Indiana or India, Pittsburgh or Peru! And, sadly, orphans are a part of every society, whether we like it or not.

Peru is no different, but Ana Dodson is.

Ana, an adoptee, started an organization called *Peruvian Hearts* when she was only eleven to improve the quality of life for children in Peru who are living in orphanages or in extreme poverty.

Of course, you don't have to travel to Peru to find orphans, poverty, hunger, sickness and despair; there's plenty of that right in our own backyard. But Peru spoke to Ana and that's where Ana went, and that's what makes her revolution different from all others.

You'll read more about Ana later in our special **Young Revolutionaries Who Rock** section, but for now know this: Ana did what many young revolutionaries do – she found something broken and was determined to fix it.

WHAT IS BROKEN?

What's broken in your world?

I ask because the first part of this book was about getting angry; I think we're all plenty of that right about now! But this second part of the book is about getting active, moving forward and getting results, so now it's time to put the anger behind us and start acting to make our world a better place, one revolution at a time.

"Broken" has all kinds of meanings to all kinds of people. For some of us, what's broken is literal: the stoplight at 5th and Elm Streets, the water fountain in D Wing or the brakes on our ten-speed. For others, the picture is a little bigger: what's broken for them may be the justice system or how many women are battered and abused each day.

Still others see the world as their home and try their best to fix what's broken in it. So they recycle to stop waste, work on initiatives to stop global warming or, as in the case of Ana Dodson, cross international borders and help orphans live better lives in Peru.

But this book isn't just about them; it's about *you*. I want you to figure out what's broken in your town, in your school, in your home or even in your life and think about how you can start putting it back together.

Here are three quick tips to help you focus on fixing what's broken:

1. **Start local:** You don't have to travel to Peru or India or even Indiana to fix what's broken. Chances are, if you look hard enough, you can find plenty that's in need of mending right where you live. Maybe your town needs a

new sign at the city line, or your street needs a sidewalk so kids can safely walk to school. Whatever it is, know that nothing is ever too small to be broken – or too big to be fixed.

2. **Start small:** Many times we get carried away and bite off more than we can chew. But what happens when we get too full and can't swallow anymore? We end up spitting the extra stuff out and giving up on most of what we started, if not the whole project. The biggest mistake you can make in waging your own revolution is giving up because you started too soon, too big or without enough understanding of how to fix the problem in the first place. Remember: you're young and time is on your side. There is no deadline or expiration date on your own personal revolution.

3. **Start somewhere:** Whatever you do, start somewhere. Even if it's just a small thing every day, like putting spare change in the children's hospital jar at the grocery store or stockpiling school supplies for needy students one item at a time, think of the impact you'd make on your world if you did that every day for the rest of your life. Think about the impact if you'd started doing that last year, or the year before. Now think about how much time and energy you will waste by not starting until next year or the year after. The great part about being a young revolutionary is that not only do we get to pick the size of the battles we fight, but the sooner we start fighting, the longer we have to fix what's broken!

67

WHY IS IT BROKEN?

Fixing something is a great feeling, but action without understanding is likely to be doomed right from the start.

There are lots of reasons why things are broken. Let's use the example from above about getting a new sidewalk on the way to school. Now, maybe a dozen other people have complained to the city about WHY they need a sidewalk in your neighborhood. And maybe the city's even doing something about it, like getting bids from contractors or analyzing their budget needs for the coming year. BUT cities only have so many dollars in their budgets, and measly little sidewalks aren't usually high on their list. No, they're much more likely to fix major roads, put more police cars on the street or fix the fleet of school buses than rush out to start construction on a brand new sidewalk for you and your neighbors.

It's kind of like you and your allowance or part-time job check: let's say you get $100 a week either working around the house or for the family business or at some other job. Out of that $100 comes a variety of your expenses, like money for school clothes, lunch money, and maybe gas for your car or insurance or movie tickets or whatnot. If you're like me, that weekly allowance goes pretty fast. And no matter how big the allowance, we always seem to spend as much as we have. So if my parents were to suddenly bump me up to $200 a week instead of $100, it might feel like Christmas came early for a week or two, but pretty soon I'd be spending exactly as much as I made each week – and always needing more.

Cities are no different. Big or small, urban or country, they have "X" amount of dollars to spend each year and a long list of things to spend it on, like putting more police officers on the street, paying the mayor's salary, keeping the red lights red and the green lights green and the phone lines up. So there may be a few dozen reasons WHY no one has put a sidewalk on your street to make it easier for kids in your neighborhood to get to school.

So... understanding why that sidewalk isn't there yet can help you get it there. How? Well, don't just fire off angry letters to the mayor or picket his office or post a parody of how he walks or talks or combs his one patch of hair over his bald spot on YouTube. Taking bold steps without having all the information can be counterproductive to your revolution, no matter how satisfying it might feel at the time. To get results – to get what you really want – put together the research first and present it to the city in a calm and rational manner. And don't forget to ask your parents or teachers for help.

Here are a few good points you might make at the next City Council meeting to back up your argument with cold, hard facts about why you need that sidewalk – and soon:

- X amount of children are hurt or killed each year walking to school
- A certain percentage of these tragic accidents could be avoided if more paved sidewalks existed
- More kids would get to school on time if there was a sidewalk
- Fewer kids would skip school if the sidewalk was there
- More kids would ride bikes to school if the sidewalk was there
- More kids riding their bikes to school would save the city on gas money for buses and maybe even salaries for an extra bus driver or two

69

I mean, these are some pretty good points. You'd be hard pressed to sit on a City Council and ignore someone's argument if they came at you with so many good, hard, factual reasons for paving a simple sidewalk.

How do you find out all these facts and figures? Start by Googling keywords like "accident" and "school" and "sidewalk" and soon you'll be able to come to the city with reasons WHY it's so important to build that sidewalk. It may not happen overnight, but the more you understand the WHY of what's broken the more likely you are to be able to fix the WHAT.

WRITE A 3-POINT MISSION STATEMENT

Every year, schools all across the country publish something called their "mission statement." You've probably seen it before, maybe in the form of a banner over the front office at your school, or sometimes at the bottom of your school newsletter or even in the margins of your report card.

They usually sound something like this: "Morgan James High School pledges to offer its students the highest quality education possible by hiring the most talented teachers available and creating an atmosphere that's conducive to learning."

Yawn, right? Well, it isn't boring to your principal, or your parents or your teachers – and especially not to the committee who spent all summer coming up with that little mission statement! Because that mission statement means action; it means the school administration doesn't just have a vague plan rattling around in their brains, but a plan for fixing what's broken, step by step.

So, instead of saying something vague like "Morgan James is great," the school has a goal and an actual published plan to reach it. They want to offer students "the highest quality education possible." How are they going to do it? By "hiring the most talented teachers available and creating an atmosphere that's conducive to learning."

All kinds of institutions use mission statements, not just schools. Big companies do, too; many of your favorite companies. Here's one I think you'll like: "To Refresh the World...in body, mind, and spirit. To Inspire Moments of Optimism...through our brands and our actions. To Create Value and Make a Difference...everywhere we engage."

Pretty cool, right? I mean, who wouldn't want to "inspire moments of optimism" and "refresh the world," right? By the way, that's not the United Nation's mission statement or UNICEF's; that's Coca-Cola's mission statement.

And here's one from another company you might recognize: "Establish Starbucks as the premier purveyor of the finest coffee in the world while maintaining our uncompromising principles as we grow." Now, I think you and I would both agree that Coke and Starbucks are two companies who go out and get things done, namely sell sodas and coffee. They achieve results by having a very specific plan; and you can, too.

We can learn something from corporate mission statements. More importantly, for every revolution we start – for every broken thing we want to fix – we should write a mission statement to remind us of why we started our revolution in the first place. Here are the three elements that every mission statement needs:

71

1. **State the *Problem*:** What is it that you intend to fix, specifically? Is it building a sidewalk? Getting a new movie theater for your town? Helping orphans get adopted? Getting kids to quit smoking – or never start in the first place? Then write it down; make it a part of your mission statement. Say, "My goal is to build a sidewalk for my street so that kids aren't afraid to walk to school." Now that is a great beginning to a super mission statement.

2. **State the *Action*:** How will you fix what's broken? In our sidewalk example, we talked about **a.)** Doing research **b.)** Gathering statistics on kids who've been hurt walking to school **c.)** Presenting this information to

the mayor. Those are three active things to do. But how will you do them? You might add this to your mission statement to make it clear: "I will gather facts and make a clear, logical presentation to the City Council at their next meeting." This is effective because not only do you state the action, but when, and that's a powerful statement.

3. **State the Result:** What happens after you've gathered the facts and made your presentation? Now come the results – and the "payoff" portion of your mission statement. So for this section you might write something like, "As a result of these actions the city will clearly see the problem and begin construction on our new sidewalk."

72

So, your three-part mission statement reads: "My goal is to build a sidewalk for my street so that kids aren't afraid to walk to school. I will gather facts and make a clear, logical presentation to the City Council at their next meeting. As a result of these actions the city will clearly see the problem and begin construction on our new sidewalk."

I think you will agree that the above sample mission statement leaves nothing to the imagination. In three short sentences we have established **a.) The problem b.) The action c.) The result**. Not bad, not bad at all.

And if I were to write a mission statement for this book, it would probably look something like this:

I would like to help fix this world, one problem at a time, by creating a generation of "young revolutionaries" who in turn solve problems in their towns, thereby making the world a better place for everyone!

Nice, huh? So let's look at the elements:

You've got the **Problem**: *"Help fix this world, one problem at a time..."*

You've got the **Action**: *"by creating a generation of 'young revolutionaries' who in turn solve problems in their towns..."*

And, finally, you've got the **Result**: *"thereby making the world a better place for everyone..."*

Short, sweet and to the point. That's effective communication; that's an effective declaration for a revolution that rocks!

How about you? What would your mission statement look like? Take the following blank lines and give it a shot. Make sure to include the three parts of your mission statement first:

73

Problem: _____

Action: _____

Result: _____

My Mission Statement:

_____

_____

_____

_____

_____

START FIXING IT

So far you've defined what the problem is, conducted research in order to understand why it's a problem, and written a cool mission statement to act as a guide as you start to solve the problem. What's left? **Start to fix what's broken.** Remember: Part 2 is all about action, so the completion of all this careful planning is to simply... start... DOING.

If you're going to do research to show your city council why you need a new sidewalk, **then start doing it.** Google key terms to find the answers to your questions, collect statistics and maybe some super quotes. Put your findings in a document and make copies for all concerned – and don't forget to cite your sources.

If you're going to protest the high starch, carbohydrate, and caloric content of your school lunches and what it's doing to your health, **then start doing it.** Find out the nutritional valuation of each meal, gather information on recommended daily dietary needs for your age group, and then tell the school board what you've learned – and how you'd go about providing more nutritious school lunches.

If you're going to start donating 10% of your weekly allowance to a charitable organization, **then start doing it.** Don't make excuses for why you can't donate the money; take a pencil to your budget and learn to get by on a little less. Sure, it may be a sacrifice, but if you really want to do it, you'll find a way so that the pleasure you derive from your charitable gift offsets the pinch to your pocketbook.

It really is that simple. Sure, you may go left when you need to go right or turn around and go back and start over, but how will you ever know until you try? All it takes is that all-important first step.

74

YOUNG REVOLUTIONARIES WHO ROCK

Ana Dodson, 16

Ana Dodson is a junior in high school who likes to read, write, paint, play golf and ride her horse named Blizzard! She is also the founder and CEO of *Peruvian Hearts*, a non-profit organization that she started when she was 11 years old.

75

Why Peru? Explains Ana: "I traveled to Peru in 2003 with my mom and a group of Peruvian adopted kids. Our group visited many orphanages while we were there and one of the orphanages was in Cusco. This orphanage housed abused and abandoned girls. The children wore tattered clothing and shoes made out of rubber tires. They had dark circles under their eyes and they were malnourished. I felt very connected to these girls because I could have been one of them if I had not been adopted by my parents and brought to America. I wanted to give these girls some of the same opportunities that I have been given."

For Ana, she had found what was broken. What's more, since she had been an orphan and knew how powerless the feeling could be, she already knew what she could do to "fix" this problem. And before leaving Peru, she had all the inspiration she needed to ACT on fixing this particular problem once she got back to the States.

"When I was leaving the orphanage one of the girls that I had gotten to know, Gloria, came up to me and hugged me and started to cry," Ana says. "She told me that she knew I would never forget them and that one day I would help them."

And so Ana did; and quickly, too. "When I got back to America, I could not forget the faces of the girls at the

orphanage," she explains. "Those girls had really touched my heart and that is why I decided I wanted to do something more to help these girls."

How did Ana get started? Well, it was as simple as opening her mouth. "I asked my parents how I could start a non-profit organization," she explains, "and finally with some discussion we soon started brainstorming names for my organization. My dad is a lawyer so he was able to do all of the legal paperwork in order for *Peruvian Hearts* to become a non-profit organization. And that was the beginning of *Peruvian Hearts*. We then started sending letters to friends and family and I started to speak to Rotary clubs, schools and groups."

Remember that mission statement I told you about earlier in this chapter? Well, turns out I'm not alone in thinking it's a great idea. As a matter of fact, Ana created her own mission statement for *Peruvian Hearts*: "The mission of *Peruvian Hearts* is to improve the quality of life for children in Peru who are living in orphanages or in extreme poverty. We do this through focusing on education, health care and nutrition. *Peruvian Hearts* has raised about $100,000, which has been used to support children living in orphanages in the area of Cusco, Peru."

See how nicely Ana's mission statement aligned with ours?

She stated her **problem**: *"The mission of Peruvian Hearts is to improve the quality of life for children in Peru who are living in orphanages or in extreme poverty."*

Then her **action**: *"We do this through focusing on education, health care and nutrition."*

Finally, her **result**: *"Peruvian Hearts has raised about $100,000 which has been used to support children living in orphanages in the area of Cusco, Peru."*

This gave Ana a guide to follow as she began doing the good work for which her charity was formed. The best part about *Peruvian Hearts* is that it isn't just a charity in name alone; it's literally helping people lead better lives every single day.

Ana proudly says, *"Peruvian Hearts* also supports about 80 children who come in each day for a meal at the orphanage in Anta and we give them vitamins. In addition, we are supporting a food program in Lamay, a small town in the Sacred Valley and we are supplying them with a monthly stipend, food, and vitamins. We are also currently looking for another orphanage that we can support."

In so doing, she has given the orphans of Cusco, Peru, something they might have never had before: hope. The hard work, effort, and action are finally starting to pay off. Recalls Ana: "Giovana, a 17-year-old girl who has spent most of her life in the orphanage that we are supporting, said she has really been able to see the difference that *Peruvian Hearts* has made in her life and in the lives of other children. It is very exciting because she is our first girl to graduate high school and she is now studying to get into University."

What advice would Ana give to other young people who want to change the world? "I would tell other young people who want to change the world to always follow your heart and to never give up in hard situations."

Are you beginning to see the common thread that runs through all revolutions?

TURN ACTION INTO AN A.R.T. FORM

Like any work of art, action is made up of several different elements. To help remind you how to act and why to act when it's time to act, I've put together another helpful acronym to show you why it's so important to act now – before it's too late: A.R.T.

A is for Attention: The first step to action – to spotting what's broken and learning how to fix it – is to pay attention to your surroundings. Maybe you're lucky and have a great life, but just because you've got it good doesn't mean that it is also true for everybody else in town. Look around and see what might be wrong where you live and see what needs to be fixed. If you live in the suburbs or a fancy neighborhood, this might mean crossing the tracks to the other side of town where more, and bigger, problems lie. Don't be afraid to inch out of your comfort zone to find out where the problems live.

R is for Ready: Don't jump until you're ready to fly. This is great advice for the would-be revolutionary. It's fine to get excited, even anxious or energetic about the revolution, but fixing what's broken means controlling ourselves first. Control means taking action only when we're ready. I can think of nothing worse than telling kids in Peru you're going to help them get adopted or ease their poverty – and then giving up on them because you "just weren't ready" yet. That's why I spend so much time talking about preparation; don't rush into any of this – there's no deadline or expiration date. Better to wait until ready than quit because you started too soon.

T is for Tenacity: Tenacity is just another word for sticking to the mission even when times are tough. Being tenacious is having that bulldog ability to grind through the rough times to get to the good. So maybe the City Council didn't think your arguments were so great after all and your new sidewalk doesn't get built right away. Most people would just shrug, say they gave it their best shot and start taking the bus, where a tenacious individual would stick to it, day after day, month after month, until that sidewalk gets built. This year, next year... or even the next; it doesn't matter when the sidewalk gets built, as long as it gets built.

■

Whatever you do, start somewhere. Even if it's just a small thing every day, like putting spare change in the childrens' hospital jar at the grocery store or stockpiling school supplies for needy students one item at a time, think of the impact you'd make on your world if you did that for the rest of your life. The great part about being a young revolutionary is that not only do we get to pick the size of the battles we fight, but the sooner we start fighting, the longer we have to fix what's broken!

■

Dallas and Mia Tyler in New Mexico

CHAPTER FIVE
I Have the Right
to Listen to My Gut

"I can confidently say that we are a generation that can – and does – make a difference. If you have a societal concern, you have the power to make a difference."

—DANIEL FELDMAN, Age 17

As kids, we are told to "listen" about a million and one times each day.

"Listen up!"

"Listen to your father when he's talking to you!"

"Are you even listening to me?"

"Do you ever listen?"

"What's that you're listening to?"

But I have a new one for you: "Listen to your gut!"

That's what Daniel Feldman did when he started the non-profit organization *Kids Feeding Kids* after volunteering at a local rescue mission. That day, Daniel decided that he would "bake a difference." Explains Daniel: "I learned that each year 13 million children in the United States go hungry or are at risk of hunger. No child should ever be deprived of the nutrition they need to live and thrive in our society."

I can think of few things in this world that are worse than hunger. Most of us don't know what that feels like. I mean, when was the last time you were truly hungry? Not just a little famished because you were late for lunch or forgot to grab a Pop-Tart on your way to school, but ravenously hungry because all you'd had to eat all day was a bowl of rice or stale bread and water – or nothing at all. And if we do feel hunger pangs every once in awhile, it's nothing compared to the bottomless hunger that deprived kids feel every day. Most of us get hungry and run to the nearest drive-thru to satisfy our hunger; other people don't have access to such luxuries or, if they do, can't afford them.

Imagine that: not enough in your pocket for something off the dollar menu. Not just because you forgot your wallet or it's the day before payday, but because you just flat-out don't have enough money to spend a dollar on food and don't know when you will have a dollar or where it might come from. At home there is literally nothing, not just nothing you want, but nothing to eat. Nothing in the refrigerator, nothing in the cupboards, nothing in the pantry, and that is if you are lucky enough to have a home. And this isn't some Third World country we're talking about here, but the United States of America. I feel guilty just writing this; with a fridge full of food if I feel faint and a freezer full of more food should that run out, which it never does because my folks shop every week to ensure there's always food on hand.

But what if they couldn't make that weekly trip to the market? What if they lost their jobs or got injured or sick and couldn't put food on the table? It isn't out of the question. Few of us are millionaires and many are just a paycheck or two away from being poor, destitute, and even homeless.

Daniel knew he had to do something to help end childhood hunger in this country, but what? Like many young revolutionaries, Daniel decided to listen to his gut and learned that organizing bake sales wasn't just something he could do, but something that every young person could do.

84

And so *Kids Feeding Kids* was born. Daniel, who attends Mainland Regional High School in Linwood, New Jersey, has raised nearly $40,000 by organizing dozens of bake sales and other fundraising activities to feed hungry children.

Think about that for a minute: $40,000 earned to date. That's more than some of the families he feeds will make in a year. Think of all the food that money has bought, how many jars of peanut butter and loaves of bread and pounds of hamburger and gallons of milk. Through his selfless actions, Daniel Feldman has put his money where his mouth is – and fed hundreds of children who would have otherwise gone hungry without his help. That, my friend, is the very definition of a **Young Revolutionary Who Rocks**!

But it wasn't always this way; before volunteering at that local rescue mission, Daniel was just another kid like you and me. Going about his business, downloading songs on his iPod, grabbing fast-food bags full of burgers and fries without another thought, never going to bed hungry or stopping to think that anyone else was, either. But the minute he saw all those hungry families lining up to be fed – so many of them with children – he knew in his gut that he had to do something. Like the rest of us, Daniel did things out of order; he didn't wait to figure out what to do before getting started.

Instead, he listened to his gut **first** and figured out what to do **second**.

85

HEED YOUR GUT-O-METER

Cars have odometers that tick off every mile that's driven. We have pedometers to tell us how far we've walked. Each of us also has what I like to call a Gut-O-Meter: that little siren in our stomachs that tells us what's right or wrong – and when to take action.

The Gut-O-Meter usually goes off when our instinct is to do something we know isn't good for us – like pocketing that candy bar instead of paying for it, or snatching a few extra bucks out of our Dad's wallet, knowing he'll never miss it, or downloading that song for free instead of paying for it, or getting the answers to the test instead of studying for it.

If you look around, you'll see everyone has a different setting on their Gut-O-Meter. Some kids wear stuff that would make your Gut-O-Meter scream; others have no problem cheating on tests, parking in a handicapped spot or sneaking an extra carton of milk through the lunch line without thinking twice.

Part of being a young revolutionary is setting your Gut-O-Meter a little higher than everybody else's. You can't efficiently lead a part-time revolution or make a half-hearted attempt; this isn't a hobby – it's a lifestyle. We may not get paid to organize bake sales, teach girls how to fight off sexual predators or give away cleft-lip teddy bears, but it's what our Gut-O-Meters tell us to do and so we do it; no questions asked and, usually, with no complaints. And the only way to know what you should do – which revolution you should start – is to listen to your Gut-O-Meter more often.

Here are some simple ways to heed the call:

Me first: We are often told to think of others first. In fact, that's what this book is all about: service. But sometimes we have to say "me first" before we can figure out the best way to serve others. Listen to your Gut-O-Meter. Only then are you capable of hearing the message that counts most: the one that comes straight from within you.

Quiet time: Life sometimes gets noisy: school, friends, activities, TV, radio, cell phones…all fill our days with noise, cutting down on quiet time to think about what we need to do – or preventing us from thinking about what is truly important at all. When you see a problem and you're trying to figure out a way to fix it, the best way to begin is to listen to your gut. And the best way to listen to your gut is to set aside quiet time.

Heads up: It's so easy to be distracted in this day and age. I have a *gut feeling* that Gut-O-Meters go off a lot more than the number of times we actually pay attention to them. But in order to start a revolution and keep it on track, you need a well-tuned Gut-O-Meter to steer you in the right direction. Pay attention!

THE GIVING EQUATION

I know this isn't a math book, but I'm going to give you an equation anyway. It's called the Giving Equation, and every young revolutionary I've ever met – and those I've read about in magazines or on the Internet – *knows it by heart*. What is the Giving Equation?

87

Brain + Heart = Gut

Let's look at the elements of the Giving Equation:

Your Brain: The human brain receives electronic impulses and sends messages to the rest of the body. You want to walk? The brain sends a message through the central nervous system to your legs to walk. You need to remember the answers to your Social Studies test? The brain's got you covered. But the brain, as awesome as it is, is only half the equation that makes up what you really are, let alone how much you'll actually give in one revolutionary lifetime.

Your Heart: The heart isn't just a blood-filled organ pumping away right now in your chest; your "heart" is also that part of your spirit that harbors judgment, understanding, forgiveness and love; compassion. Your heart is that part of you that cries at Hallmark commercials and quivers when you see long lines of poor kids getting to school early to line up for free breakfast in the cafeteria or waiting for a pair of free shoes at Christmas. But like the brain, your heart is also smart: it knows that the spirit residing in you comes from the same source as the spirit dwelling within me and every other person. The heart knows that – at the level of spirit – We are All One. Ultimately, this is the reason why young revolutionaries do what they do: in helping others they are helping themselves.

Your Gut: Did you know that in order to make a 3-D movie filmmakers actually shoot the movie twice? Not one after the other but at the same time, using two special cameras for every frame and shooting side-by-side. Only when the two images are superimposed does it become 3-D and you need those nifty glasses to see it. Like 3-D movies, your gut is literally the best of both worlds: it has all the wisdom of your brain and all the compassion of your heart, and when the two are superimposed your gut gives you the "real" message you should be listening to. After all, if we only listened to our brain, we'd have no heart; no compassion or caring. But if we only listened to our heart, we wouldn't be using our brain; we'd act naively and probably make a lot of dumb mistakes. But our gut takes the signals from our brain and our heart and combines them to process the signals coming straight from our soul! (No funky glasses required.)

The more often we follow the Giving Equation, listening to our gut gets easier and easier because we can trust where the messages are coming from. You can accept the logic coming from the brain that says things like, "Check with your parents first before giving all of your life's savings to the homeless shelter downtown" or "You can't save all the kids in Peru today because you don't even have a passport yet!"

You can also process the messages from your heart that say things like, "I can't believe I only gave $5 at the animal shelter today when I had twenty bucks in my purse" or "I should really give half my birthday presents away to the homeless shelter; I have so many things already!"

But your gut – the "referee" who makes the calls when your brain and heart are in conflict – processes both messages and guides you toward making the right decision at the right time.

In conclusion, it takes guts to be a **Young Revolutionary Who Rocks**!

YOUNG REVOLUTIONARIES WHO ROCK

Daniel Feldman, 17

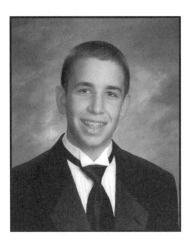

Kids Feeding Kids: what a great idea! I was thrilled when I first heard about it, and couldn't wait to interview the mastermind behind this non-profit organization that takes the awesome power of kids and the simple goodness of a bake sale and turns it into a clever cure for world hunger: Daniel Feldman.

Daniel is seventeen years old and about to become a high school senior. In addition to being on the crew team, Daniel is active in the 4-H Youth Council and spends every extra minute he has volunteering to help others in need. Daniel is an active, eager and ambitious **Young Revolutionary Who Rocks** in every sense of the term.

But what was the thing that set Daniel's Gut-O-Meter off and encouraged him to start such a worthwhile organization as *Kids Feeding Kids*? Well, let's go straight to the source:

"Each year twelve million children in the United States are hungry or at risk of hunger," warns Daniel. "Every fourth person standing in a soup kitchen line is a child, and hungry children are more likely to get sick and be absent from school and suffer from reductions in physical growth and impaired

90

brain function. My volunteer effort focuses on this important issue. My motivation is rooted in my belief that no child should ever be deprived of the nutrition they need to learn and thrive in our society."

Daniel's gut told him he needed to do something about feeding these hungry kids, but what? Like many young revolutionaries, he got his start early: "Recognizing the severity of global poverty, my youth volunteer group focused our international efforts on assisting the rural children of Ghana, West Africa," Daniel explains.

"Although I anticipated hunger to be a problem in this third world country, I was astonished when I learned about the severity of hunger in America. Right here in my own community, the local food pantry shelves were empty and children were waiting in soup kitchen lines to get their first meal of the day. In a country so wealthy that just didn't make sense. I decided that I could make a difference. By raising funds and awareness about childhood hunger, while educating youth about the importance of nutrition in their learning and development, I believe I can be instrumental in creating a hunger-free America."

But what, exactly, could Daniel do to raise funds and awareness? As awesome an idea as *Kids Feeding Kids* was, Daniel had to start somewhere. "I began by participating in hunger walks," he says, "organizing food collections and volunteering at my Community Food Bank. Simultaneously, I began working with the Share Our Strength Great American Bake Sale (GABS) program. I built on my interest in baking and changed a hobby into a talent for helping others.

"I founded the Peer Partners project *Kids Feeding Kids*, which is a fundraising and hunger education effort. The goal of *Kids Feeding Kids* is to help end child hunger in America. In addition to participating in food collection drives, *Kids*

Feeding Kids organizes bake sales throughout the year as well as creative entrepreneurial efforts, including the creation of a 'Baking Book' and limited edition anti-hunger pins designed to raise both awareness and funds that provide nutritional meals to children who might have otherwise gone unfed. *Kids Feeding Kids* strives to educate others regarding the importance of nutrition on normal growth and development and why ending child hunger in America is essential."

Over the years Daniel has raised nearly $40,000 to help feed children all over the country, to say nothing of the countless volunteer hours he's devoted to organizing and attending bake sales wherever and whenever he could. Here is a guy who actively lives his Revolution 24-7-365. Remember how I said that revolutions can be addictive? Daniel Feldman is living proof; the guy is practically a bake sale guru!

Daniel recalls the first time he realized his efforts were making an active difference in someone else's life: "One of the most touching experiences I've had was at my first full scale bake sale on the Ocean City Boardwalk. It was a balmy night with thousands of people strolling the boardwalk, enjoying all the wonders of the evening. Standing beside Masiela Lusha of the *George Lopez* show, who came to support my event, we observed a young woman rummaging through her pockets trying to gather enough change to buy her children a cookie. We immediately recognized that this mother and her three small children were the exact people that we were striving to help with this fundraising event. Responding quietly and gently we offered the children their choice of cookies. They all enjoyed a special treat that night and the smiles on their faces have since remained imbedded in my mind and secured in the forefront of my motivation to continue the fight to end child hunger."

But here's what Daniel is not telling you, and what maybe those three small kids don't even realize themselves yet: it was more than just a cookie; the cookie each child received that night was a gift – a true gift from the heart – and gifts like that don't come along often enough. They should (we can all bake a cookie or donate a dollar), but they don't. I have no doubt that because of Daniel's unselfish act that night, a mother and her three children will one day give back in more ways than you, I or Daniel can possibly imagine.

If there is a true ripple effect we as **Young Revolutionaries Who Rock** ever make, it is this: giving is a good act that sets off a chain reaction of other good acts. The gift keeps on giving because those who receive it get something much more valuable than a bear, a meal, or new clothes: hope. And that hope is passed along time and again as the ultimate gift worth sharing; it is contagious.

As Daniel Feldman shows, it doesn't take much to improve another human being's life. A cookie and a smile... these are the simple tools Daniel Feldman used to start his own rockin' revolution.

What tools will you use?

Where will you start?

93

WHAT ARE YOU GOOD AT? (COME ON, DON'T BE SHY!)

Daniel Feldman is good at baking. I am good at street fighting. Claire Crawford is good at raising money to buy *"Claire's Bears."* But what are you good at? Can you sew? If so, you might start a non-profit that mends clothes so that kids don't have to spend so much on back-to-school shopping or so that their hand-me-downs don't look so rundown.

Can you sing? Do you dance? Maybe you can throw karaoke or dance parties to raise funds for the charity of your choice. Maybe you excel at sports or spitting watermelon seeds farther than anyone in town or maybe you are a world class competitive eater and can down more chicken wings or hot dogs than anyone on the planet. Maybe you're a great organizer.

In a later chapter you'll meet a kid who changed the world by making over 2,000 basketball free throws. So no matter what you're good at – kicking soccer balls, sewing, spitting watermelon seeds, break dancing or eating 30 hot dogs in five minutes – you can turn your talent into making a difference.

And since we're more than halfway through this book, I think now is the perfect time for you to have a little "me time" and figure out just what it is you can do. Now, remember, you'll have friends enlist in your revolution, so you won't be fighting the good fight alone. But what you will do alone, at least in the beginning, is start up your revolution in your own special way. And that means making a decision about what, exactly, you aim to do – and that has a lot to do with what you like to do; what you're good at doing.

So use the blank space I've provided to rack up some points in the skills department by listing all of your talents:

Things I Know I'm Good At

_____   _____

_____   _____

_____   _____

_____   _____

_____   _____

WHY GUT MATTERS

We're kids; I get that. But it's almost easy to forget how young we are when in the company of so many kids doing such mature things as stopping smoking, educating kids in India, helping orphans in Peru, feeding the hungry, or caring for those with cleft lips. This is heavy stuff, no doubt about it, but all of these initiatives were started by kids still in their teens; some of them before they had even reached thirteen!

95

So what does listening to your gut have to do with any of this stuff? Simple: every young revolutionary we've met so far started somewhere – a bake sale, a free throw, a fundraiser, an idea on a scrap sheet of paper – and that starting point was an inkling, a whisper, a thought or a notion that they could be – they should be – doing something about *this*.

"This" changes for every kid. For one young revolutionary, "this" was making sure kids with cleft lips had a teddy bear to cling to before, during and after surgery. For another, "this" was stopping kids from taking up smoking. My "this" is different; your "this" is different.

What isn't different is THIS: every young revolutionary starts with a rumbling in his or her gut; a feeling of injustice, of anger, of disappointment, of sadness, of fear – a glimmer of an idea that tells you deep down in your gut, "Hey, something's not right here. I can't just walk away and let this be."

It could be the sight of a homeless family sleeping on the street and how that image lingers with you as you get ready for bed that night, how you still think about it the next morning over breakfast, or go out of your way to pass by the same street to see if they're still there, sleeping in their cardboard box.

And once that inkling, that feeling, that nagging gets stuck in your gut, well, good luck getting rid of it! That becomes your THIS, and trust me: THIS is hard to get rid of. You will think about that family – your "this" – throughout the weekend, whenever you hear a sad song or a happy one, watching TV or reading a book or taking a jog or taking out the trash. It's gonna be hard having a good time knowing that there's a family suffering on the streets where you live.

Time will pass, that homeless family will move, and your thoughts may move on to next Tuesday's biology test… but the gut remembers – for as long as you listen to it, that is. It's only when we stop listening to our gut that we stop being **Young Revolutionaries Who Rock**.

Those who listen to the gut are the ones who do something about THIS.

■

Listen to your Gut-O-Meter. Only then are you capable of hearing the message that counts most: the one that comes straight from within you.

■

Dallas with Penn Badgley of *Gossip Girl* at the *Teen Choice Awards*

CHAPTER SIX

I Have the Right
to Change the World

"Teenagers often feel that they can't make a difference;
that their voices will not be heard. But over the past four
years, I have learned that with discipline and motivation,
anybody can affect change. All young people should know
that they have the power to realize their dreams."

—NIHA JIAN, Age 19

In the movies, changing the world usually means
stopping 100 nuclear bombs from going off at once, blocking
a gamma ray from the Death Star or wiping out all the killer
zombies in town with a turbo-charged weed whacker.

In real life, it's actually a whole lot easier. As we have
seen throughout this book, all it takes to change the world
– one revolution at a time – is the vision, strength and stick-
to-it-iveness of one plucky kid who refuses to back down
from a fight.

When eighth-grader Niha Jain decided to do a school
report on domestic violence, she never imagined it would
change her world – let alone ours. As part of her research,
Niha visited the local YWCA Family Violence Shelter. There
she got to see firsthand what it means to be abused, betrayed
and abandoned by those you love most.

Having never toured a women's shelter before, Niha
was shocked; in this case, shocked into action. Seeing how

much the shelter helped those who live there, she was doubly shocked that many were forced to wait for a free bed. Worse, the shelter wasn't exactly a place anyone would want to call home; not just yet anyway.

But Niha thought she might be able to do something about that. She explains: "The YWCA Family Violence Shelter was not in good condition when I toured it. Parts of it were filthy; there was a shortage of cleaning supplies. I was so moved that I started a cleaning supplies drive at my middle school, collecting 300 items for the shelter. It was a small start, but it helped the YWCA immensely, and it motivated me to continue helping."

Today Niha is set to enter Harvard University and take her first steps in the world of adult education. But she has already seen more – and done more – than most adults twice her age, and it all started in eighth grade with that first visit to the YWCA Family Violence Shelter.

What's going on in your world?

And what can you do to change it?

WHEN IT COMES TO CHANGE, LESS IS MORE

I love that Niha's first steps toward Revolution involved going to her school and gathering cleaning supplies for the women's shelter. What a great way to start: simple, easy, collective. Hers was an immediate, active and practical response; she didn't spend a bunch of time debating how it should be done or when to start – she saw a need and responded. The shelter was filthy; she had a gut feeling how to change that. She went to school, started a revolution and did something about it.

And that's how simple, how quick, how effective and how practical change can be: a scrub brush in one hand, a bottle of 409 in the other; grab some friends, grab some mops and away you go.

Revolution, here I come!

Here's the thing about Change: you have to make it personal. If there's a common thread that ties together all of our **Young Revolutionaries Who Rock**, it's that they picked a charity, cause, or problem that set off their Gut-O-Meter. Regardless of the cause – the perils of smoking, helping the homeless, or feeding the hungry – young revolutionaries wage a war that for them is intensely personal. As in Claire's case, she helped ease the fears of children with cleft palates because she was born with a cleft palate. In Chad's case, he waged a war against smoking because lung cancer had taken his grandfather's life. And Ana rescued orphans in Peru because she, too, had been an orphan.

I love that with all her brainpower, popularity, charm and charisma Claire Crawford is still sticking with *Claire's Bears*; still staying with that basic premise of raising funds, buying bears and passing them out to as many kids with cleft palates as she can. She's not hangin' at the mall; she's found her cause and – like any good young revolutionary – she's giving it everything she's got. All her focus, all her energy, her spare time and every last cent goes into the *Claire's Bears* Revolution – and she's changing the world in her own special way, for as little as ten dollars at a time.

When it comes to revolutions, less really IS more.

ONE CAUSE, ONE REVOLUTION, ONE YOUNG REVOLUTIONARY

Let's face it: there is no shortage of causes. If you really stop to think about it, it's amazing our world keeps on spinning. Between global warming, economic upheaval, the real estate crisis, the price of gas, rising murder rates, natural disasters, bad news and worse news, it's a wonder any of us get out of bed in the morning, let alone go about our day as if the sky wasn't falling.

Look in any direction and there's something worth fixing: a homeless shelter, an AIDS clinic, recycling, food for the hungry, and clothes for the needy. These are all worthy causes, but how many can you handle effectively before you burn out?

If you try to change too many things, especially big, scary things, you'll end up frustrated, disappointed and defeated. Like my Dad says every time another envelope comes in from some charity I pledged money to on the phone because I just couldn't say no, "I know you want to help everybody, Dallas, but we can't help *anybody* if we go broke!"

And he's absolutely, 100% right. What if Claire started giving away bears for everything, from broken arms to stomach aches to acne to amputees? These are all worthy causes (I'm sure everyone could use a little comfort in dealing with acne). But pretty soon, she'd have to raise more and more money and she wouldn't be able to spend the time, care and attention she gives to the cause she's so passionate about – cleft palates – because suddenly she's fighting twenty revolutions instead of one.

But look how many of us have found one thing to change – just one – and made the world a better place for it. Remember, less really IS more when it comes to **Young Revolutionaries Who Rock**; do one thing but do it to the very best of your ability. Be a five-star chef that caters to an exclusive customer / cause rather than a short order cook trying to feed the world and coming up woefully short.

So when it comes time to pick your revolution, choose wisely. Look for things you know you can do; not things you know you can't. For instance, if you're not a basketball player, then attempting to set a record by shooting 3-point baskets for a local charity probably isn't your best course of action. But you *could* organize a tournament of local ballers to make the jump shots while you tally up receipts from pledges for every basket. In fact, this could be an easy way to jump start your own revolution!

Before you get started, here are a few questions to ask yourself, pre-revolution:

- Is this something I feel comfortable with?
- Is it something I can stick with for the long haul?
- Is this something I can keep up with?
- Is this something I can do in my spare time?
- Do I have friends, family and support to help me?

SEE CHANGE, THEN BECOME IT

Remember: change is personal. You don't just change the world; you change yourself in the process. It's literally impossible to help someone else and NOT be helped in return. So make sure it's a journey you want to start before you take the first step.

103

Remember: not everybody can travel to India and teach school there. Not everybody can feel comfortable getting up in front of Rotary Clubs and asking for donations so they can buy $10 teddy bears for kids with cleft palates, no matter how worthy the cause. That doesn't mean those people are better or worse than you; just different.

Don't feel bad if you're shy, nervous or hesitant; these are things that will change as you begin to change the world. Maybe you don't need to speak in front of a hundred people just yet. Maybe you start out by going to the people you know and telling them what you're trying to do, and ask them for help: one neighbor, friend or family member at a time. Start small, but start.

After all, starting small is still a start and that's the really important part.

One thing I've found is that the young revolutionaries I've talked to all really enjoy what they do. They must love it; some of them have been doing it since they were eight or nine years old and are now in college.

Some of them have been doing it for years, week in and week out – every summer, weekend and holiday vacation – and they're still inspired about what's going to happen next; they still have plans for next summer, next year and after college. That is the type of passion, purpose and commitment needed to change the world.

So if your revolution turns into a chore or too big of a challenge, how long do you really think you're going to keep it up? Better to start a revolution you're committed to rather than just going out and doing something because you think you have to or feel guilty because you're reading about what everyone else in this book is doing. Make it personal, make it powerful and, most of all, make it something you are passionate about.

In other words, see the change you want to become – then become it!

FIVE STEPS TO CHANGE

Like most things in life, change is a process acquired over time. If you've ever tried a new diet, a new exercise program, a new class or beauty regimen or even the latest style of clothes or hair color, you'll agree with me that it takes time to get used to change.

You don't just wake up one morning and suddenly run 6 miles, eat cold oatmeal for breakfast and dye your hair purple. You gradually ease into it, like sticking your foot in the shallow end of a cold pool and slowly sinking until your head is covered. Once you've adjusted, the water feels great; but the shock of diving in head first can sometimes take your breath away.

And you know by now that I'm always ready with a helpful bullet list or a few tips to smooth the transition. So to help you ease into the change that is coming, I've come up with five simple steps that transform change into a lifelong habit:

1.) **Slow and steady wins the race:** Change takes time; this much we already know. Even little things like losing those last ten pounds or pulling your GPA back up after a slack junior year can be a gradual process. But for social change to happen — to feed the hungry or clothe the needy or get your neighborhood to recycle — it can take weeks, months and even years. Remember, we're still kids! We've got our whole lives to wage revolutions wherever we see fit, so whatever we do now is just a prelude for the huge change to come.

2.) **One step at a time:** Have a plan and stick to it; that's how real change occurs. Remember how you layered your mission statement in three stages: **problem, action** and **result?** If you want to raise money for teddy bears to give to sick kids, don't just leave it at that; it's too nebulous an idea. Instead, be specific: write down how many bears you'll need, how much each bear will cost, your likely sources for getting the money, how much each person will need to donate, a list of kids to receive the bears, etc. In movies, change happens overnight or, more often, in handy little three-minute montages set to majestic music, where the boxer **miraculously** gets in shape, the alcoholic **immediately** gives up booze or the

105

homeless guy **suddenly** wins the lottery and cleans up his act. In real life, change is rarely miraculous, immediate or sudden, which is why it's so important to plan carefully and bring about change one step at a time.

3.) **Passionate, powerful and purposeful:** If the change you want to make is going to be permanent – and if you're going to be in it for the long haul – it must be passionate, powerful and purposeful; these are three key ingredients for any revolution. In other words, you should feel **passionate** about what you're doing. It should rock you to the core and cause you to jump out of bed every morning, ready to start another day, fight another fight and win another battle. If you don't, you'll never feel that burning desire you need to stay the course. The change should also be **powerful**; it should affect people in a way that truly changes their lives – like a safer, cleaner womens' shelter or a campaign to stop kids from smoking or a teddy bear that looks just like you and is waiting for you when you get out of surgery. You can't do it just to make yourself feel good; it should be powerful enough to make others feel good as well. And it must be **purposeful**; it should be realistic and active and not happen by accident, but because of steps you've carefully taken, goals you've set and accomplished on purpose. When we combine passion, power and purpose the revolution is bound to be successful because it's built on a solid foundation.

4.) **One thing, every day:** It's not the big things you do once in awhile but the small things you do **every single day** that make for effective change. So if you're going to bring about change, do something about it **every single**

day. Revolutions aren't fought on weekends or over the holidays; they are won by gaining ground inch by inch, day by day. Every day is valuable and you can't afford to waste a single one. Send a letter, buy a stamp, walk a mile, give a speech, give a dollar, write an email, find an address, send another letter, send three more emails, start a petition, join a club, donate your time, ask a question, fill out a form, meet a mentor, write your Congressman, call a reporter, review a good book, write the author, write your own book, etc. They don't all have to be big things, but change happens **every day**. To make the changes we want, we have to do more, not less.

5.) **I mean it – EVERY day:** It bears repeating, so let me say it again: saying you'll do something every day is easy; *doing* something every day is hard. Trust me, I know. But change is worth the effort. So buy a calendar, one with big, fat squares for each day of every month. For every day, write down in its square what you're going to do and **then do it**. That's why it's best to start small – mail a letter, write a chapter, start a food drive – so that you can find satisfaction with each accomplishment. It will feel great crossing off each goal, no matter how big or how small. Remember: little things done every day can ultimately change the world, but only if you do them EVERY DAY!

YOUNG REVOLUTIONARIES WHO ROCK

Niha Jain, 19

When it comes to **Young Revolutionaries Who Rock**, Niha Jain is already a highly decorated veteran. Since eighth grade she's been volunteering her time at the charity she founded, *Generation United to Succeed (GUTS)* – formerly known as the YWCA Youth Board.

In the fall of 2008, Niha entered the freshman class at Harvard University. That's over four years in the trenches – and through every year of high school – creating major change. That's enough to keep any high school student busy, and Niha has the stripes to prove it. She explains: "I currently serve on the Nestle Very Best in Youth Foundation Board and the America's Promise Youth Partnership Team. I also work with the organization I founded, *Generation United to Succeed (GUTS)."*

GUTS began on that fateful 8th grade trip to the local YWCA Family Violence Shelter. As Niha recounts: "Domestic violence affects millions of women and children worldwide, and I wanted to tackle that problem in my own community. I founded the YWCA Youth Board, a service organization for high school girls to help battered families staying at the local YWCA Family Violence Shelter. In addition to raising money and supplies to help the shelter, the YWCA Youth Board focused on increasing youth volunteerism and leadership. Although young people often feel they cannot make a difference, the YWCA Youth Board worked to change that by spearheading youth leadership summits in our community."

Adults ran the local YWCA Family Violence Shelter and adults lived there. But it was Niha, then an eighth grader, who instigated a positive change in the lives of these battered women and their small children – and it all started with some simple cleaning supplies; a mop, a broom, a sponge and a can of Comet.

A cleaning drive! It sounds so simple – and it is. Imagine the kinds of drives you could run at your school: food drives, recycling drives, clothes drives, school supplies drives – the list is endless and just waiting for you to explore. But as Niha cautions, it was plenty of work; work that was both rewarding and plentiful.

109

"When I initiated the cleaning supplies drive at my middle school, I was happy to see such a positive response from my peers – lots of students were eager to help. I realized that involving more people in service projects would also cause a greater impact. In my sophomore year of high school I founded the YWCA Youth Board to make a bigger difference and to motivate other youth to volunteer."

But Niha wanted more; and now that she had a little experience in raising funds and awareness in her community, she decided to kick her revolutionary activities up a notch. She explains: "To help the YWCA, the Youth Board collected 300 travel bags because battered women often enter the shelter with little more than the clothes on their backs. We have worked extensively with the YWCA After-School Program, where we tutored underprivileged children, organized Halloween and Christmas parties for them, and collected 1,000 books to motivate them to read.

"For Celebration of Women's Week, the Youth Board partnered with the local sheriff to organize a free self-defense class for women in the community. For two years at Christmas, the Youth Board donated stuffed animals to children at Shriner's Hospital. In August 2006 and 2008, we spearheaded

the *GUTS* Youth Summit, motivating hundreds of high school students to become leaders. We have raised about $5,000 for the YWCA Family Violence Shelter, the American Cancer Society (Relay for Life), the *GUTS* Summit, and for sending snakebite anti-venom kits to impoverished villages in India, where thousands die of snake bites annually."

For all the good Niha has done, it's the personal moments that stand out most:

"When helping the Family Violence Shelter," she says, "I was not allowed to meet the battered women and children in order to protect their identities. Many of them, after fleeing their homes, are still pursued by their abusers. However, I have mentored girls on the YWCA Youth Board, and I've watched many of them grow into leaders. I have observed shy girls become outspoken as they organize service projects. It is very exciting to see these girls become empowered and realize their own potential to make a difference."

The way I see it, that's how Niha could describe herself!

PARTING WORDS ON CHANGE

The beautiful thing about change is that you don't just change yourself, you transform others. And those others? Well, they often turn into young revolutionaries themselves. The movement feeds on itself, a circle of life, going round and round and picking up more and more people along the way. You help one person, they help one person, that person helps another person, and soon the whole community is helping each other, one act of kindness at a time. It may sound corny, but it's true. If only more young revolutionaries would step up and bring about change in their communities, I'm convinced more people would follow their example in becoming revolutionaries.

It's like being a recruiter without the hard sell: you start by picking up clothes or raising money or handing out teddy bears or teaching girls self-defense and in every recipient of your good acts there is a change that says, "Hey, I can do that. Someone took the time to help me; it's my turn to take the time to help somebody else."

And they do; they do it all the time. I've seen it with my own eyes and other young revolutionaries can tell you the same: good leads to good and change leads to change. It is working; there just aren't enough of us to go around – yet.

If you're still not sure, just ask yourself this simple question: "What do I have to lose?" Seriously. Right now the world is the pits! Violence, crime, tragedy, betrayal, disappointment and loss of home and hearth and health and hope everywhere you turn.

So if the grownups and the government and the politicians and the corporations and the bigwigs aren't doing enough to right these wrongs, what do you have to lose by trying something different and making a difference for the better? Do you think I'm making all this up? Can you deny the money these kids have raised, the good they've done, the lives they've changed and the positive impact they've made on a negative, depressing, disappointing world?

I hear kids complain all the time how the world is just too big to change, the problems too massive and the numbers too intimidating. And they're right; the world *is* big, the problems *are* massive and the numbers *are* intimidating.

But we can do something about them together – you and me and all the other **Young Revolutionaries Who Rock**. And it doesn't take much; you've seen how little it takes to make a person happy, feed the hungry or cheer up a kid who's sad or sick or orphaned – some cleaning supplies, a teddy bear, a bake sale.

It's not rocket science, it's simple arithmetic: you help one person and they help one more and they help one more and soon the ripple effect spreads goodwill and cheer farther and faster than any government program. And we aren't even

112

talking about the adults who get inspired when they see kids doing stuff like this and decide they want to get in on the act as well.

I can't tell you how many adults have come up to me at speeches and seminars and workshops and told me some fantastic service effort they're planning to do as a result of what I have already done. I get emails from adults all over the world who have held their own *Just Yell Fire* programs in their communities or at their kids' schools. Some are at libraries, some at a local safety conference; some are even having *Just Yell Fire* parties for their daughters' birthdays or graduation. They watch the movie and then practice the moves. One girl said it made her feel great to know that she might be the reason her friends won't become victims of sexual assault when they leave for college.

Revolutions touch everybody; men and women, boys and girls, rich and poor, young and old, black and white – you and me.

Right now the world is not working very well. I knew it when I wrote a book called *Young Revolutionaries Who Rock*; you knew it when you picked up this book and bought it. I mean, if we were living in a utopia there wouldn't be any need for revolution. And I'm not going to say that the secret to a long life and great happiness is contained in this book, but I will say this much: all the **Young Revolutionaries Who Rock** that I've met and you've read about are happy, productive, peaceful, prosperous people.

The Bible says that we should live by the Golden Rule: do unto others as you'd have others do unto you. But if the whole world was full of **Young Revolutionaries Who Rock** there would be no need for *Young Revolutionaries Who Rock*! (And that's a good thing, because it would mean all the revolutions had been fought, won and settled peacefully.)

I'm not naïve enough to say "Pay it forward" and leave it at that. The revolutions we start will take hard work – and plenty of it. The problems *are* huge, but so are the numbers of people willing to help – if only we lead the way. There are six billion people on this planet and if half of us decided to make a change, most of the world's problems – probably *all* of the world's problems – would be solved tomorrow.

Isn't that worth starting your own revolution today?

■

When it comes time to choose your revolution, choose wisely. Look for things you know you can do; not things you know you can't. For instance, if you're not a basketball player, then shooting baskets for a local charity probably isn't your best course of action. But, you could organize a tournament of local ballers to make jump shots while you tally up receipts from pledges for every basket. In fact, this could be an easy way to jump start you own revolution!

■

Just Yell Fire movie set, Parking Lot

Part Three

FIGHT FOR YOUR OWN PERSONAL BILL OF RIGHTS

Olympic Gold Medalist Dominque Dawes and Dallas at the *Huggable Hero Awards* in Washington DC

CHAPTER SEVEN

I Have the Right
to Help Others Who Can't Help Themselves

"Having leukemia has taught me to be a better person;
more caring and selfless. I have learned that I am able to
educate and inspire people to step up and help others by
simply telling my story. I know that if I can help make a
difference at my age, then everyone else has the power
to make a difference as well."

—Pat Pedraja, Age 13

In Part 1 of this book we got angry; in Part 2 we
learned to **help ourselves.** In this – my favorite part of the
book – we learn to **help others.** Because, really, that's what
Young Revolutionaries Who Rock is all about. I mean, you can't
have a revolution for one, right? No; it's about helping others
while helping yourself in the process.

Did you know that it's much harder for minorities to find
bone marrow donor matches if they need a transplant to help
cure things like leukemia? That's right; according to the New
York Blood Center, "Caucasians in need of a bone marrow
transplant have as much as an 80% chance of finding a match
through donor registries, but for minorities the percentage
drops dramatically."

Pat Pedraja didn't know the statistics, either, but he
knew he had leukemia and that one day he might need a

bone marrow transplant. While recovering from chemo and radiation when he was only ten years old, Pat saw a story about an African-American woman with leukemia who was in desperate need of a donor.

She never got one, unfortunately, and weeks later she died. Pat was devastated to learn of such a preventable death and – like all **Young Revolutionaries Who Rock** – decided to do something about it. What he did has changed the way minorities find bone marrow donors and, in the process, saves lives. It's not every young revolutionary who can claim to save lives, but Pat is one of the lucky few who can say so and I think you'll be jazzed when you read his story and learn more about how he started his own medical revolution.

You'll read more about Pat later in this chapter, but I wanted to introduce you to him now because he's such a great example of what it means to fight for your right to help others who can't help themselves – and help yourself in the process.

It's okay to help yourself. When I started this book I asked the question, "What's in it for me?" I think by now you've seen how much our young revolutionaries get from giving, but one of the biggest returns they get on their investment is goodwill; the feeling of positive peace that comes over them when they've affected a life, changed a life or, in Pat's case, even saved a life. Helping others really is about helping ourselves, and I can tell you personally that there's no greater combination.

THOSE WITH GREAT POWER HAVE GREAT RESPONSIBILITIES

There's a great line in the first *Spiderman* movie where Peter Parker's uncle tells him, "With great power comes great responsibility." I recall that line each time I write about one of these young revolutionaries; kids who realized how good we all have it – and how most people don't.

I'm amazed each time I read a new story or finish an interview with one of these great kids. Take Pat, for instance. Here's this young guy with leukemia, recovering from severe radiation and chemotherapy treatments, sick most of the time, nauseous, sore, uncomfortable and stuck in some hospital bed while all his friends play hockey and baseball without him.

And what's he thinking about?

How to help people less fortunate than him!

When it comes right down to it, no matter how bad we think we have it, if we were to actually look around at our lives – the sweet bedrooms, the fancy iPods, the home computers, the allowance, the closet full of clothes, the silly complaints about curfew and bland school lunches and too much homework – we'd realize how good we have it compared to just about everybody else on the planet.

A lot of people don't have it so good: not in Darfur, where violence is common; not in Cuba, where freedom is stifled; not in Afghanistan, where bloodshed is a daily event and innocent victims get caught in the crossfire; not even in America, where hunger, homelessness and poverty are more common than most of us would care to admit.

People are abused, hurt, scared, threatened, bullied, hungry, poor, and thrown out of their homes daily; the world is a scary place for a majority of people, and the only way to make it less scary is to step up and help those who can't help themselves.

It really is up to us, you know. With all its red tape, political correctness, bills and addendums and referendums and rescheduling, the government is a body that's slow to move and even slower to help. But we are young, fast and

121

free. We can start a fundraiser or collect clothes or canned goods or cleaning supplies for charity, and *boom*; it's done.

We set up in the gym before school, during lunch or after school, maybe set up a table to get signatures or donations, post a sign or two, and we're in business. What did that take, a single school day? And in the time it takes to watch a movie we can collect hundreds of cans of foods, piles of clothing and bags of cleaning supplies. No bills to pass, no petitions to sign, no taxes to pay; just gathering from the fortunate and giving to the less.

At the end of the day, that's all a revolution really is: someone in a position to help making the effort to help; not second-guessing themselves, not worrying if it's going to affect their popularity or what their friends might think, just stepping up and lending a hand where it's needed most.

We have it good, you and I; lots of people don't have it so good.

If we don't help them, who will?

3 REASONS TO HELP

Sometimes it can seem like a dog-eat-dog world out there. I mean, when was the last time someone stepped up, smiled, opened their heart and did something *really nice for you*? When was the last time anybody lent you a dollar for lunch or gave you a ride home when the bus was late or even held the door open as you were rushing for the elevator? I know it can seem hard and lonely and brutal out there, but is that any reason why you should turn around and treat the next guy the exact same way?

Bad manners are a lot like yawning; they're rude, unsightly and contagious. You get the door slammed in your face enough times, you figure, "Why should I hold the door open for anybody else? Nobody ever does it for me."

But just think of yourself as the deciding factor; the line in the sand between being selfish and being helpful. If you keep doing the right thing and living by the Golden Rule – doing unto others as you would have them do unto you – you just might be the person that makes other people reconsider their actions.

You hold the door open for one person, and maybe – just maybe – they think twice about slamming it in someone else's face the next time they have the opportunity. You give that homeless vet at the red light some spare change from your coin box and, who knows, the next three people waiting for the light to turn green might give him even more.

Sure, today it's just holding open a door but tomorrow it could be something much bigger, like starting a scholarship fund for needy students. The difference between bad manners and good is often a smile instead of a frown; a "yes" instead of a "no." But if you don't hold the line and stick to your guns, you're not being part of the solution – you're part of the problem.

123

I was flown to Washington, DC, to receive the National Caring Award and I was also inducted into the Frederick Douglass Museum Hall of Fame for Caring Americans. WOW! What an honor, especially considering the fact that the first recipient of this award was Mother Teresa. Can you imagine what it feels like to be in the same category with Mother Teresa? Talk about cool!

The only reason I bring this up is because my absolute favorite thing ever is a meditation written by Mother Teresa. In fact, I framed it and keep it on my wall where I can see it every day. I thought I'd share its inspirational message with you. Here it is:

People are often unreasonable, irrational, and self-centered.
Forgive them anyway.

If you are kind, people may accuse you of selfish, ulterior motives. Be kind anyway.

If you are successful, you will win some unfaithful friends and some genuine enemies. Succeed anyway.

If you are honest and sincere people may deceive you. Be honest and sincere anyway.

What you spend years creating, others could destroy overnight. Create anyway.

If you find serenity and happiness, some may be jealous. Be happy anyway.

The good you do today will often be forgotten. Do good anyway.

Give the best you have, and it will never be enough. Give your best anyway.

—MOTHER TERESA OF CALCUTTA

124

If the teachings of Mother Teresa are not enough to encourage you to do the right thing, maybe the following three reasons *will* be:

1.) **If you don't, who will?** So many people wait for someone else to make a change or do what's right, but if you wait long enough, pretty soon nobody rises to the occasion – even when it's life or death. Did you see the video of that poor woman keeling over in the emergency room while everyone ignored her and minded their own business while she died on that waiting room floor? Doctors say she might have been saved if she had gotten medical treatment sooner. So if one person – just one – had raised an alarm or gone over to her, she might be alive today. Oftentimes, people are just waiting for someone else to make the first move. Why can't that person be you? Why can't you be the one to hold open the door, give up your seat on the bus or walk over and check on someone who's just slumped over onto the floor? If you make the right move, others *will* follow. Trust me; it's what revolutions are all about.

2.) **You've got great examples:** If you need motivation next time you're wondering whether or not to do the right thing and help somebody else who can't help themselves, just turn to this book. It's full of **Young Revolutionaries Who Rock**; great examples of kids who did the right thing, whether it was convenient or cool or not. And the best part is they aren't doing it to win some popularity contest – and they're certainly not doing it for the money. Every kid you meet in this book is an unpaid volunteer. No, these young revolutionaries are doing it for one reason and one reason only: it's the right thing to do and they're in a position to do it.

3.) **Good things come back to you:** Do you believe in payback? Karma? Fate? Blessings? I do. In fact, I believe that when you do good things for others, they come back to you – and then some. Call it karma, call it fate, call it payback – call it what you will – but the best way to see if it's true is to find out for yourself. Trust me, you *won't* be disappointed.

YOUNG REVOLUTIONARIES WHO ROCK

Pat Pedraja, 13

126

Pat Pedraja is 13 years old and going into the 8th grade. He loves sports, especially baseball and hockey, and his bulldog 'Rinkles. But Pat is lucky to be alive, let alone become an eighth grader. He explains: "I was diagnosed with leukemia when I was 10 years old. I spent most of the first year in the hospital going through painful chemotherapy and radiation." Ouch; anyone who's ever had chemotherapy and / or radiation can tell you just how painful it is: harsh chemicals speeding through the body, nausea and vomiting, soreness and pain, weakness and potential anemia; the patient too tired, upset or nauseous to eat; it's no walk in the park.

Spending nearly a year in the hospital is enough to bum anybody out; but not Pat! Instead of burying his head in comic books or fiddling with his Gameboy, he had other people in mind. Particularly those people who, like him, had leukemia but who, unlike him, wouldn't have as easy a time finding a donor as a young white kid.

Pat recalls: "One day when I was in the hospital I saw a TV show about an African-American woman with leukemia who desperately needed a bone marrow transplant. The show explained how there was a critical shortage of minority donors on the National Marrow Donor Program Registry.

"A few weeks later I learned that the woman died when she couldn't find a match. I am half Cuban, and realized that one day it could be *me* searching for a match! I didn't want anyone else to die when they don't need to, so I decided to start a National Marrow Donor Drive called '*Driving for Donors*' to add marrow donors and save lives."

Now that's a **Young Revolutionary Who Rocks**!

What did Pat do next? "I worked really hard to educate myself about marrow donation and how people can join the National Marrow Donor Program (NMDP) Registry. I had to raise money to pay the tissue typing fees for people to join the registry and so I sold ads on my bald head. In order to start my drive I had to find an **RV** and sponsors, plan out a tour, work with 40 donor centers around the U.S., and advertise our drives!"

127

Hats off to Pat – or should I say, hairs off? Selling ads on your bald head, now that's something most kids would be self-conscious about. But not Pat; he saw it as a way to help, as a way to raise donations for people in need. And did he ever!

Pat was off to a great start, but he couldn't do it all alone. He needed more **Young Revolutionaries Who Rock**. Luckily, he found them – and then some. Recalls Pat: "As people heard about my efforts they would email me with heartbreaking stories of people they knew who were desperate for help. It showed me how cancer has affected so many lives. So far I've held drives in over 38 states and 3 countries and added over 10,000 new marrow donors. My drives have found 4 matching marrow donors for people in need. I won't find out about the success of the marrow transplants for another year, but I know that these people have families that love them and the second chance at life means the whole world to them."

Some young revolutionaries rock by helping raise money for their favorite charities, others by making other peoples' lives a little easier every day. Kids like Pat Pedraja are actually saving lives.

And you could save lives, too!

NEXT TIME, IT COULD BE YOU

The thing about helping those who can't help themselves is that one day it could be you who needs help. Who's to say we won't be the ones needing a bone marrow transplant tomorrow? Or what if a hurricane, tornado or earthquake leaves you homeless and the bank ATMs are out of order and you can't get money to buy food and have nowhere to go?

Wouldn't you want someone helping you then?

There's this guy we see on the corner most days; he's at the same stoplight 9 to 5 most weekdays, walking from car to car, looking hungry, tired and desperate. Sometimes we give him money; sometimes we don't have the change to give. Some people help him out; most don't. Some even honk at him and wave him away.

So often it's easy to think of the homeless as, "Oh well, if they can write a sign that says they're homeless, they can go out and get a job." But there's more to it than that; there always is. And even if there isn't, who are we to judge?

What if your dad lost his job and your mom had to work fewer hours? What if they lost all their investments and couldn't afford a mortgage anymore? Most people in this country are just a few paychecks away from being homeless. I'm not trying to spread doom and gloom here, but if you think that getting cancer, being in an accident or even losing your home can't happen to you, think again.

Then where would you be?

We're all on this great journey together and the only way to make it through with a little hope, decency and grace is to get together and help each other along the way. Being a **Young Revolutionary Who Rocks** is the best way I know to start.

129

Dallas surprised by *Huggable Heroes Award*

■

*If you need motivation next time you're wondering whether or not to do the right thing and help somebody else, just turn to this book. It's full of **Young Revolutionaries Who Rock**; great examples of kids who did the right thing whether it was convenient or cool or not.*

■

Dallas, Jennifer Stone and Selena Gomez of Disney's
Wizards of Waverly Place at the *Teen Choice Awards*
in LA

CHAPTER EIGHT

I Have the Right
to Fight for My Own Rights
– and the Rights of Others

"Kids shouldn't wait until they're older to make a difference. They shouldn't wait until they are an adult. They should make a difference now. We are the coming generation – we are the generation that will change the world for better or worse. We need to start today."

—AUSTIN GUTWEIN, Age 14

Centuries ago our forefathers fought for our rights to live free in this country. They gave their lives so that we could be free to worship as we please and live our own lives on our own terms. Sometimes, looking around today, it's hard not to think they'd be disappointed in how we turned out.

Oh, we live free and on our own terms, all right, but then what? Do we help each other or mind our own business? Do we do what's right or what's easy? Do we care where all the trash goes or just keep piling it on? We say we want to "go green," but most of us do so with a bag of garbage in one hand and a gas can in the other. Sadly, when it comes right down to it, most of us have a "me first" attitude and leave it at that.

But not 14-year-old Austin Gutwein. As Austin points out: "I am really a pretty ordinary kid who just loves serving people. I have been raised in a Christian home and taught that I should care for others."

Well, Austin might call himself "ordinary," but I call him a **Young Revolutionary Who Rocks**! (And after reading his story, so will you.) You see, Austin was watching TV one day when he saw a news story on African children with AIDS. Probably millions of kids – not to mention adults – saw the same news story, but Austin got a gut feeling and decided to put down the remote and actually do something about AIDS in Africa.

So he pondered the problem until he came up with a great idea: instead of having a walk-a-thon where people pledged donations for every step he walked, Austin – who would much rather shoot hoops than take a hike – had a "basket-a-thon" where sponsors pledged so much money per basket he sank.

Little did sponsors realize what a crack shot Austin was on the basketball court. In fact, on World Aids Day 2004, Austin went to his school's gym and shot 2,057 free throws to represent the 2,057 kids who would lose their parents during that school day. Not only did he raise awareness for the desperation and devastation that AIDS was causing in Africa, but he raised money for every single basket!

I love Austin's story so much because of all our **Young Revolutionaries Who Rock** I think his revolution was the simplest of all; just shoot baskets. That's it. Take a stand, make a statement, raise some funds but do what it is that you enjoy, dedicate the effort toward helping others, and your revolution can be joyfully successful.

Austin's story shouts down all those doubters who think they could never do anything to help, that the problems are too big or that you need to be a celebrity, politician or millionaire to actually make a difference in this world; you don't. Austin's story proves that in order to start a revolution all you need to be is a caring kid with a cause and a basketball; that's all.

How could a revolution get any simpler?

SOMETIMES YOU HAVE TO FIGHT FOR WHAT'S RIGHT

Can you believe 2,057 kids lose a parent to AIDS every single day? I can't; Austin can't, either. He did something about it when lots of others didn't. And that's the thing about **Young Revolutionaries Who Rock**; they're there when you need them.

No matter what the cause that needs fighting for or the broken thing that needs fixing, you can believe that our generation of media-savvy kids is going to be on top of it. We process our information instantly and the minute something touches us we respond.

I think that's why there are so many kids doing so many great things, now more than ever; we're the only ones who seem to know what's going on. And the **Young Revolutionaries Who Rock** keep getting younger every year.

It doesn't matter how old they are; most of the kids I've met, interviewed and profiled in this book weren't even teenagers when they started their own personal revolution and the rest are just graduating high school now.

It doesn't matter how big you are. Most of these kids are average in size and, in fact, when Austin first tried out for the basketball team he got rejected! But that didn't stop him from trying again – in more ways than one.

And none of the kids profiled in this book were rich, well-connected or even famous when they started their revolution. They were just normal, everyday, average kids like you and me.

Once upon a time I thought the government handled all problems, the police figured out the rest and the firemen

135

came when they saw flames. But life is more complicated than that, and getting more complicated every day.

While some people hack on the government and the police, the fact is their jobs aren't easy and become progressively harder with every new challenge society throws their way. Sometimes it's not enough to wait for a bill to pass or for a program to get funding or for the cops to arrive. Sometimes private citizens have to stand up and fight for what's right even if it's so that the government – or ordinary people like you and me – take notice. That's what being a revolutionary is all about: taking matters into your own hands when nobody else will.

What Austin did in starting his own private revolution was to raise awareness for a problem very few of us knew about: African children orphaned by the AIDS epidemic. Since then his story has been covered by MSNBC, all the major networks, and newspapers around the country. He's even a star on YouTube, and he did it just by shooting baskets.

But it wasn't easy. If he had shot 50 baskets, do you think anyone would have noticed? Austin knew he had to send a message that particular World AIDS Day, and he knew that 2,057 was the magic number.

Why? Because it stood for something; that number had meaning, significance and power. It wasn't just baskets in a gym or numbers on a chalk board. That huge number – 2,057 – represented the amount of parents who die from AIDS every single day and beginning with that message – with a basketball – Austin literally changed the world.

YOUNG REVOLUTIONARIES WHO ROCK

Austin Gutwein, 14

The great thing about Austin Gutwein is that he really is what he says he is: "a pretty ordinary kid who just loves serving people." What makes Austin tick? It's simple, really: "I have been passionate about helping kids who have been orphaned by AIDS and I am trying to turn the tide on AIDS."

137

Now, a lot of kids are passionate about things but don't know what to do about them or where to start. Austin was like that, too – at first, anyway. "I started to imagine what life would be like if I had lost my parents and what I would have to go through," Austin says. "I put myself in these childrens' place and realized I should do something about this problem."

But what should he do? What *could* he do? And how? Turns out, the answers weren't that far off. Austin remembers: "I got started by asking my parents what I could do to make a difference. I was only nine at the time. My parents didn't know of anything a nine-year-old could do, so they put me in contact with World Vision and I talked to a man there who said, 'Why not use your favorite sport to make a difference?'

"I decided that I would play basketball to help these kids. It would work just like a walk-a-thon except I would shoot hoops instead. So on World AIDS Day 2004, I went to my school gym and shot 2,057 free throws to represent the 2,057 kids who would lose their parents during my school day."

So simple, yet so effective. And what happened next showed Austin, and the rest of the world, that shooting baskets really *could* help save lives. "People sponsored me and we were able to raise almost three thousand dollars," explains Austin. "That year, the money was used by World Vision to provide hope to eight orphans."

One of the great things I've learned from interviewing all of these **Young Revolutionaries Who Rock** is that they just don't stop after they've met their goal. It's like they're constantly reaching the finish line and then pushing it back so they can get more done.

138

Oftentimes, they're starting a whole new run altogether. Whether it's the built-in Gut-O-Meter that makes them start a revolution in the first place or the change that's brought about once the battle has begun, young revolutionaries just can't seem to let go of the dream.

Take Austin, for example; since 2004, he hasn't looked back. "From that year forward," he explains, "thousands of people have joined me in a basketball shoot-a-thon called *'Hoops of Hope.'* By doing something as simple as shooting free throws, *Hoops of Hope* participants have raised over $450,000. The children left behind by AIDS now have access to food, clothing, shelter, a new school and, finally, a medical testing facility.

"Last year, our goal was to raise $150,000 to build a medical testing lab in Sinazongwe, Zambia. This lab will enable medical staff to test parents for HIV/AIDS. The medication will allow parents suffering from HIV/AIDS to prolong their lives and keep their children from joining the 15 million children already orphaned by this disease."

$450,000! Now that's a revolution that worked, and in more ways than one; more than money and awareness was raised by Austin and his *Hoops of Hope* campaign – he has actually saved lives.

One revolution – and one basket – at a time.

139

Austin and AIDS caregivers in Africa

IS THE FIGHT IN YOU?

Fighting is something we're taught NOT to do in school, but I don't think "fighting for your rights and the rights of others" is what our teachers have in mind when they warn us to stay out of fights. In fact, when it comes to kids like Austin Gutwein and all the other **Young Revolutionaries Who Rock**, I think every teacher I've ever had would agree that they should keep on fighting, no matter what the odds.

And that's the question I have for you: is the fight in you?

Is there something you care about so much you're willing to give up your free time, your weekends, your evenings, your summer vacations and plenty of parties? Is there something – *anything* – you're so passionate about that you're willing to put yourself on the line and act on its behalf?

So far in this book you've seen kids fight for the rights of minorities to get bone marrow transplants, come to the aid of Indian children in need of modern educational facilities, rally kids orphaned by AIDS, feed the hungry, and provide shelter. Every young revolutionary we've seen rock these pages so far has fought for one thing or another: money, time, compassion, funding or respect.

What would you fight for?

And what are you waiting for?

■

Centuries ago our forefathers fought for the right to live free in this country. They gave their lives so that we could be free to worship as we please and live our own lives on our own terms. Sometimes, looking around today, it's hard not to think they'd be disappointed in how we turned out.

■

Dallas with Washington Attorney General
Rob McKenna

CHAPTER NINE
I Have the Right
to Fight for My Own
Personal Bill of Rights

"The reality is that anyone can do it, and in fact it is really easy! My advice is to stick to it, and try new things. Dream big, and go for bigger and better every time. And never let anyone say you can't do it."

—JEREMY DIAS, Age 24

Here we are: our last chapter together. Along the way we've met some incredible kids, heard some unbelievable stories, and understood just what it means to turn inspiration into reality and not only make the world a better place but actually **save lives in the process.**

When it comes to **Young Revolutionaries Who Rock**, Jeremy Dias has been rocking long enough and loud enough to make legal history! Because of the color of his skin and sexual orientation, Jeremy faced extreme cases of discrimination by students, peers, teachers and even school officials. At 17, he began a legal case against his school and school board, and at 21 he won Canada's largest human rights settlement ever. Jeremy used the money to found *Jer's Vision: Canada's Youth Diversity Initiative* and the *Jeremy Dias Scholarship*.

But now it's time to talk about the most important young revolutionary of all: you.

That's right; this is the part where the rubber hits the road, all the excuses stop and you decide for yourself just how willing you are to step out of your comfort zone, pick a cause and fight for its right to be recognized.

What? You thought I was writing this book for my health? Oh no; you're not getting off that easy. You and I have come this far together and now it's time for you to start pulling your own weight. You've seen how easy it can be to start a revolution – shoot a basketball, collect some cleaning supplies – so now there can be no excuses for why your revolution can't start right now.

So, What Will It Be?

Earlier in this book I encouraged you to look around your neighborhood, sniff out what might be wrong and figure out a way to do something about it. Maybe you've done that already; maybe not. I'm not here to judge. Maybe your revolution has already begun; maybe it won't happen for a month – or even a year.

144

But if I can ask you for one thing it would be please don't let your revolution wither and die before you perform a single act of kindness for our troubled world. That's it; just one thing. You've seen how simple – maybe not how *easy* but how *simple* – it can be: basketball hoops, a teddy bear, a fundraiser, a bake sale.

We can do this; you and me and every other **Young Revolutionary Who Rocks**. You only have to pick a cause and go for it. I know it sounds easy, but it isn't; you and I both know life doesn't always work out as planned.

But if we stick together, if we all pitch in, check in on each other and help each other out, we can do this thing; we can change the world, one revolution at a time – but only if we get started; only if we choose a cause, plan the revolution and take action.

So I'll ask you one more time:

- What can you fix in your neighborhood?
- How might you go about it?
- Who can you get to help?
- How much will it cost?
- And…what's stopping you?

YOUNG REVOLUTIONARIES WHO ROCK

Jeremy Dias, 24

Young Revolutionary Jeremy Dias knows how to fight the system – and he has a history-making legal settlement to prove it. Jeremy Dias was born in Edmonton, Alberta, and grew up there until moving to Sault Ste. Marie, Ontario, where he attended high school. As a youth, he was motivated by social and political inequality to take action, volunteering with numerous organizations and charities. In high school he started and led a number of clubs, including Stop Racism and Ontario Students Against Impaired Driving. He also founded and coordinated the first regional Lesbian Gay Bisexual Transgender Questioning People (LGBTQP) youth group in Sault Ste. Marie.

Jeremy has been featured on Canada AM, Much Music, CTV News and CBC News, and has been a keynote speaker at countless conferences and events. He is completing a Hon. in Psychology and Political Science at the University of Ottawa, and continues to volunteer for a number of organizations. Jeremy currently serves as *Jer's Vision's* Executive Director, proudly carrying out the *Jer's Vision* mission.

Where did Jeremy get the gumption to take on Canada's legal system – and win? Not surprisingly, he had a little help from his mom. Says Jeremy: "At an early age my mother taught me that we were different because of the color of our skin. She said, 'Because of this, society will look at you differently, so you will have to work twice as hard to get half as much.' This is the reality not just for visible minority youth, but also women, LGBTQ people, many religious communities, persons with disabilities, and countless other marginalized communities and intersections of them."

As a result of his skin color and life choices, Jeremy endured bullying through most of his schooling. But a new opportunity for his father's career gave him new hope of being accepted. Jeremy recalls, "When we moved to Sault Ste Marie, Ontario, I was just entering high school. A new school, new town, new province... it seemed like the perfect way to start over and put old memories of being bullied to rest."

But his hopes for a fresh start were soon dashed when the bullying started up almost immediately. As Jeremy recounts painfully, "On my first day of school, as I put new binders and a lunch into my locker, a fellow student cornered me and pushed me against the open door. He slammed his fist into the next locker, grazing my face, and the echoing sound drew a crowd. He announced, 'Look everyone, we have us a nigger in our school.' I took a deep breath, hoping he was just kidding. I said, 'Well, I am actually a Paki.' The kids around us laughed, but before the tension could ease, he leaned over and whispered, 'I am going to kill you for that.'

"Scared, I ran away, raced down the hall, and pushed the door of my principal's office open. Carefully he put a bottle of red wine under his desk, as a wave of cabernet wafted across the room. At that moment I realized I wasn't in grade school anymore.

"In one breath I said, 'I-was-just-attacked-and-he-said-I-am-going-to-die.' He smiled politely, as he led me out the door saying, 'Well son, boys will be boys.' He almost patted me on the head as he walked into his office, and closing the door I heard the distinctive 'click,' which locked me out.

"After that, school only got worse. Think of any high school teen drama on TV and the kid that got bullied in it. Think about what happened to him, because it happened to me.

"One time, someone put paper and lighter fluid in my desk and tried to light it while I was sitting there. Another time, I found some of my books burned from small fireworks that were lit in my locker. And I can't count all the times I got name-called, threatened, pushed around, or was goaded into a fight.

"Of course, to make things more interesting, later that year I came out of the closet. Some 'friends' took the liberty of announcing it over the intercom. I guess the rest heard it through gossip.

"Needless to say things just got worse. And it wasn't just the students; some teachers were mean, too. One math teacher failed me even though I had the same answers and work as my friends. Another forced me to do a presentation in front of the class even though another student had just spit in my face. She refused to let me wash it off; I had to use my sleeve.

"I realized I had two options: live with it or do something about it. I chose to do something."

Jeremy realized he had no choice; he had to start his very own revolution, but how? Jeremy hoped that by becoming part of the system he could break down racial and gender stereotypes from within.

Recalls Jeremy: "I realized that a lot of this had to do with the fact that many people had never met someone like me, let alone interacted with them, so I got involved in sports and clubs. People met me and stereotypes were broken down. Then I started clubs to address racism and sexism and impaired driving. Soon I was the head of numerous clubs and the organizer of countless events/activities, and people started to understand that I was not just a 'colored-gay,' but rather a student and an activist and more.

"Still, despite my success, the school's administration and the school board would not let me do anything to address homophobia. I was banned from starting a Gay-Straight Alliance, denied the right to put up rainbow flags and stickers, stopped from handing out information to students and faculty, forbidden to promote the community LGBTQP youth group that I started, strongly recommended not to go to prom with my partner, and the LGBTQP books my mom bought for the library were thrown out.

"So, after trying to work with them I decided to sue them through the Ontario Human Rights Commission and I won. I used the award money to start a charity and now we work with youth across the country to support their diversity initiatives."

You might think Jeremy's story is an isolated one but, in fact, it's fairly common; Jeremy chose to do something about it – and won. He explains, "The reality is that my story is far from unique. Youth experience bullying, social isolation, violence and worse in high schools, post-secondary institutions and communities. Heck, I even got gay-bashed in University. Some studies indicate that discrimination is responsible for up to 90% of the incidences of bullying, name-calling and violence in schools and new studies are published daily about how discriminatory communities and workplaces can be. We as a society have reached a crossroad where we must choose what we are going to do about this problem."

Jeremy has good advice for future revolutionaries: be prepared to spend a lot of time, tears and effort making your dreams come true. He warns: "It took several years and tons of work to win the case against my school and school board. But I did, and when I got the letter saying that they would make systemic changes I was excited. At the board level, all the schools had to undergo major changes, including diversity training for staff, new books for the library, policy revisions and much more.

"I, on the other hand, got a check for $5,000. My mom wanted to go to Cuba, my dad said the family could use a boat, and my brother screamed 'DISNEYLAND.' I said that the money belonged to the programs and services that I never got, so in an effort to support the kids like me who want to do something, I started Canada's first scholarship fund for youth who work to promote diversity in schools and communities in Canada.

150

"I was overwhelmed with the support I got, but then something happened that I never expected: I got letters, emails, and phone calls from youth across the country and some from across the world who wanted more. They said they wanted the charity to create resources and tools for youth. Over the next two years we developed new programs and services, did research studies and also explored what was going on in other communities. The end result is *Jer's Vision: Canada's Youth Diversity Initiative*. Our mission is to work to address discrimination and promote diversity through supporting youth initiatives in schools, post-secondary institutions and communities.

"What makes our programs and services special is that we are completely youth-run. Adults serve on an Advisory Board to help with fundraising, promotion, taxes and legal matters. However, all programs and services are researched, designed and developed, delivered and implemented by youth."

"Additionally, we are unique because of our approach. We engage straight youth to address homophobia, men to address sexism, and non-visible minority youth to address racism. We still work to empower marginalized youth, but we also recognize the importance of working with the general population and bullies. Today, *Jer's Vision* has over 40 programs and services divided into several different groupings. All the programs and services are offered free of charge, and in both French and English."

I think one of the most inspiring things about Jeremy's story is his generosity of spirit and sense of forgiveness. He explains, "I decided to get involved because I believe that people are not born to hate; hate is something one *learns*. As such, hate can be un-learned, through education and dialogue, outreach and understanding. I also consider myself lucky. My parents have always been supportive of everything I have done, and always wanted the best for me. I am proud to have had a variety of opportunities and privileges that give me the ability to do what I do."

It wasn't easy, but along the way Jeremy has seen his work come to life in real-time as he conducts workshops and gives speeches throughout the country. "As we entered a school one day to do an anti-homophobia workshop, the teacher took me and another presenter aside. 'I have to warn you,' he said with a concerned tone, 'one of the boys you are about to present to has beaten up youth in two high schools because they were gay. In fact that is why he is in my class.' I remember smiling and telling him not to worry, while at the same time I was so nervous."

"As the presentation started the young man asked a few questions, but it was after, when the young man approached my colleague and I to say, 'I have to tell you something: I used to pick on fags.' He paused a second, 'I mean, people like you. Anyway, I want to do something.'"

"Within a week he started his school's first Gay-Straight

Alliance club, and by the next week was an active member in the Regional GSA Network. Today he lobbies Members of Parliament, and educates them on the importance of diversity legislation."

I'm pleased to say that Jeremy hasn't ended his revolution yet – and has no plans to stop anytime soon. He even has some more great advice for future **Young Revolutionaries Who Rock**: "The reality is that anyone can do it, and in fact it is really easy! My advice is to stick to it, and try new things. Dream big, and go for bigger and better every time. And never let anyone say you can't do it."

MY OWN PERSONAL BILL OF RIGHTS

Did you know that when you write a book, it's not really finished until it's printed, bound, shipped and sitting on a shelf in a bookstore near you? I sure didn't. I thought you worked hard, wrote all the chapters, sent it in and then waited for the five-star reviews to come in!

But nope, there are these pesky little things called "rewrites" where someone called an "editor" at some publishing house tells you things like "this is wrong" or "that is a little too mushy" or "you already said this" or "maybe cut down some on the exclamation points!!!!" (Okay, I'll give them that one!)

Well, now I'd like to help spread the joy by letting you do a little rewriting of your own. You see, the Table of Contents to this book is my Bill of Rights for kids all over the country; that's right: MY Bill of Rights.

But what about yours? Maybe you have some different ideas for what might be included there, for adding more, taking some away or simply replacing them all with concepts more conducive to your own revolution. For instance, instead of having the right to "Listen to My Gut" you'd rather have the right to "Live My Own Life." Perhaps instead of having the right to "Help Others Who Can't Help Themselves" you'd rather have the right to "Personally Challenge Politicians Through Open Debate."

Well, put pen to paper; now is your chance to do a little rewrite of your own and create **Your Own Personal Bill of Rights**. That's right; my very last chapter for you and what do I do?

Assign you homework!

But it's more than just homework. This is YOUR Bill of Rights; something you can live by, adhere to and – as you grow up and life changes and your priorities shift – rewrite over and over again.

So have at it; your own personal Bill of Rights awaits:

153

My Own Personal Bill of Rights:

Right # 1: _____

Right # 2: _____

Right # 3: _____

Right # 4: _____

Right # 5: _____

Right # 6: _____

154   **Right # 7:** _____

Right # 8: _____

Right # 9: _____

■

*We can do this; you and me and every other **Young Revolutionary Who Rocks**. You only have to pick a cause and go for it. I know it sounds simple, but it isn't; you and I both know life doesn't always work out as planned. But if we stick together, if we all pitch in, check in on each other and help each other out, we can do this thing; we can change the world, one revolution at a time, but only if we get started.*

■

Dallas with Brenda Song of the *Suite Life of Zach and Cody*

EPILOGUE

Together We Really
CAN Change the World

"Don't hesitate. If you don't take the first step to pursue your goals, then you have no chance, but as long as you take that first step, the probability of succeeding exists."

—JASMINE PETRO, Age 18

I started this book by saying that revolutions aren't always fought by the many, but more often they are fought by the few. I suppose I should clarify that a little bit as we wrap up our time together; they are *started* by the few but every revolution, at some point in time, needs to enlist a whole army of people to help it thrive.

Take our last **Young Revolutionary Who Rocks**, Jasmine Petro. I chose to include her in the Epilogue because she does something amazing: she teaches other young revolutionaries to rock. That's right; she is a volunteer who spends all of her spare time training other volunteers to, well... to volunteer! In essence, her revolution is to spark hundreds of other revolutions by helping create a generation full of **Young Revolutionaries Who Rock**!

And for good reason: there are simply too many things to be done: too many forms to fill out, emails to send, phone calls to make, petitions to spread, money to deposit, cleaning supplies to buy or bears to deliver – for one person to do it all alone.

I couldn't have made my *Just Yell Fire* film if it hadn't been for the professionals, the director, camera man, sound man, grip, special effects makeup artist and the students at the local community college who mentored me, worked for free, and volunteered their time and energy and expertise. It took five very long days, fourteen to sixteen hours each, to film the movie. Not to mention friends who showed up to be extras in the movie. On any given day there were 30 to 150 people on the set. Feeding everyone three meals a day plus snacks and drinks would have cost a fortune, but local restaurants and stores donated everything we needed. Everything! It was amazing.

We would have never gotten as far as we have if companies like Integra Telecom hadn't been generous enough to donate the server and bandwidth so that any girl anywhere in the world could download the movie for free.

And I couldn't keep the movement going today if my Mom and Dad didn't keep my schedule organized and book the speaking gigs and training sessions, and if there weren't a few dozen volunteers helping them in turn.

Remember: every general needs an expert staff of officers to keep the operation running smoothly. And the best part about any revolution is how you'll attract many like-minded soldiers who want to help.

Trust me; we revolutionaries stick together and I'm sure all of the other revolutionaries will tell you how people who believe in their cause come out of the woodwork to help.

To be sure, one of the best parts about every revolution is the people you help along the way; the lives you save or mouths you feed or comfort you give or money you share. But another huge part of keeping the revolution going and feeling satisfaction every day is the people you work alongside with as you're feeding the hungry and giving that comfort and raising that money to share.

Some people give their time, some are more comfortable giving money and others lend their expertise, like Lorraine Elias, who takes extra special time to help us design our brochures, newsletters, etc. Hillary Clinton says it takes a village to raise a child; I say it takes an army of volunteers to fight a revolution!

YOUNG REVOLUTIONARIES WHO ROCK

Jasmine Petro, 18

Most of my **Young Revolutionaries Who Rock** are mainly known for one thing: *Hoops for Hope, Peruvian Hearts, Kids Feeding Kids,* and *G.U.T.S.* The list goes on and on. But Jasmine Petro is going beyond the one-stop route by being a **Young Revolutionary Who Rocks** that trains other **Young Revolutionaries Who Rock**.

I'll let her explain: "Growing up half-Taiwanese and half-German, I have embraced my identity and celebrated many diverse cultural activities. The common denominator of these activities has always been community service, which I believe transcends differences between people. One activity that further introduced me to the world of community service was pageantry.

"In 2004, I was Miss Jr. Teen San Francisco 4th Runner Up; in 2005 I was Miss Teen Chinatown 1st Runner Up and Charity Princess; and in 2006, I was Miss San Francisco Outstanding Teen as well as Miss California Outstanding Teen 1st Runner Up. In March 2005, I raised $13,000 for tsunami survivors by approaching small businesses for donations. In October 2005, I raised $12,500 over two days at the Autumn Moon

Festival in San Francisco's Chinatown by soliciting donations in Mandarin.

"In November 2006, I helped raise $55,000 for the Asian American Cancer Support Network through the Hatwalk charity fashion show, and I was on the cover of the organization's charity calendar. For the 2008 Hatwalk, I was the official spokesperson for the Asian American Cancer Support Network. In April, I was one out of 81 people in North America to carry the Olympic torch in the San Francisco relay.

"In the days following the Sichuan Earthquake, I worked with Chinese for Peaceful Unity and 21 other organizations to put on a charity concert to raise funds for the victims of the earthquake disaster. I brought my Olympic torch to bring a little hope into the lives of those families who were deeply affected by the disaster.

"In one night we raised over $40,000. Collectively, I have raised over $200,000 for various causes and have performed over 2,300 hours of community service. CBS-5 and the *San Francisco Chronicle* celebrated my work and leadership with the Best Buddies Club – an international organization that seeks to enhance the lives of individuals with disabilities by forming one-to-one friendships – by giving me the Jefferson Award. Governor Schwarzenegger presented me with the first ever 'Governor's Academic Award.'

"This year I won over twenty scholarships, and I am a National Coca-Cola Scholar and a Regional Toyota Scholar, as well as a Build-A-Bear Workshop 'Huggable Hero.' On May 29th, 2008, I graduated from Hillsdale High School as valedictorian and on the following night, I graduated from the College of San Mateo with my Associates of Science degree in mathematics. I will be the director of the Best Buddies Program at Stanford University when I begin my freshman year in the fall.

"At Stanford University, I will be engaging in Structured Liberal Education for the first year, as I enjoy discussing ethics and learning about all different kinds of philosophies. Thoreau inspires me with his works such as *Walden* and *Civil Disobedience*, and like Thoreau, I wish to live deliberately."

Deliberate living – what a great way to put it. Jasmine Petro certainly has lived deliberately. Look at her long list of accomplishments – and for someone so young. And like many **Young Revolutionaries Who Rock**, Jasmine has pledged a lifelong fight against one thing: apathy!

She says, "I DON'T CARE!!!!'…'WHATEVER'… Apathy amongst my peers seems to be an incredibly insidious problem to me. Students that I knew had great potential to do anything they put their minds to wasted their talents as they went about their lives, not noticing the world around them and pondering the source of their unhappiness.

"Some of my peers turned to alcohol, marijuana, and other forms of destructive behavior – yearning for a new feeling, one that was not of boredom or listlessness, but rather excitement and fulfillment. While I understand that sometimes people can get really wrapped up in their own personal lives, I believe that the key to happiness is truly caring for others.

"When you spend time thinking about the needs of other people, you don't have the time to dwell on the negatives in your own life. Furthermore, when you are appreciated for your work, you feel a little bit of accomplishment that is inspiring – and this recognition motivates you and keeps you hungry to do more for others."

For Jasmine, there was no all-of-a-sudden epiphany or "magic moment" that turned her into a **Young Revolutionary Who Rocks**. It was more of an everyday thing. She recalls: "Everyday observations of my peers at school – I could just see that people were not happy and they were looking for something that would make them so. As I said, the ways they were trying to satisfy a kind of emptiness within themselves were destructive and detrimental to their mental and physical health. Watching people coming to school drunk and high just made me sad because they were spiraling into a vicious cycle that could be difficult to get out of."

"I knew that the source of my own happiness was my involvement in community services. I wanted to share this

163

Jasmine and the Olympic torch relay team

source with my peers and empower them to make the most of their talent and potential. I feel that the youth of our nation can be the most powerful agents of change, if they only cared and had the passion to pursue it."

Jasmine's path led her not to do one thing and one thing only, as a lot of young revolutionaries do, but to make her revolution *every* kid's revolution. "Having experience with diverse volunteerism and fundraising," she remembers, "I thought to myself, 'What can I do to share my experience with my peers?' The answer came to me in the form of two massive projects. I decided to design an event to reach out to the students at my school and show them how many different opportunities exist in the world of community service."

"After giving them an initial taste with the Volunteer Fair – in which I invited many non-profit organizations to share periodic volunteering opportunities, I wanted to perpetuate a

Dallas and Jasmine with Huggable Heroes awards

164

virtuous cycle by providing a formidable resource that could help students get involved periodically. This resource is now known as the *Student Run Volunteer Center (SRVC)*. Every month, I bring a group of students to a different community service activity. I reach out to students who may have never tried or thought of volunteering before and ask them to give it a try."

"Every month I organize one or two volunteer events: one big event where all members are invited and one periodical event. When I find students who are very excited about volunteering, I open up new and sustainable opportunities for them. For example, I brought some students to help the Liver

Center at Stanford University with Hepatitis B screenings – which they do every two weeks."

I love Jasmine's advice for other **Young Revolutionaries Who Rock**; it's so inspiring to me personally, and I hope it will be for you as well, as I end this book on a hopeful note. "Take each step of the journey of enacting change with passion," Jasmine suggests, "and remember that every bit of your effort is appreciated by somebody – even if you may have never met them before. Remember that the choices you make define the meaning of your existence, and it is up to you to be able to empathize in difficult situations and keep an open mind when making crucial decisions."

DON'T FRET:
THE OTHER
YOUNG REVOLUTIONARIES WHO ROCK
HAVE YOUR BACK!

Jasmine proved that helping others start their own revolution can be YOUR revolution; she's shown us that every little bit helps the movement. Another great thing is that the more people who see you fighting your revolution, the more they'll be inspired to fight alongside you in a revolution of their own.

It's more than a chain reaction; it's a nuclear reaction. Do you remember that one insurance company's commercial where the guy with the headphones is getting ready to walk out into traffic and get hit by a bus, but at the very last minute a woman grabs his arm and yanks him back? And then they go back in time and show a bunch of different, unrelated people all seeing each other do good things throughout the day. One lady opens the door for another one, one person helps a waitress avoid spilling her tray, another sees a man giving up his cab to the lady in line behind him; this lady is the one who ends up saving the guy in the headphones from getting plastered by the bus.

My point is when you see people doing good you start thinking to yourself, "Hmm, if that person can do it, why can't I?" I can't tell you how many girls have written me over the years to tell me how they've started their own revolution; just by spreading a message and leading by example, we can recruit people we've never even met to start revolutions of their own – one giant ripple effect of revolutions!

Why do you think I wrote this book? I knew I couldn't change the world all by myself, so I decided to recruit a few million volunteers, one reader at a time. You do what you do, I'll do what I do, and if we all stick together, we *can* change the course of history.

The 1980s were about luxury and laziness; the 1990s were about greed, money and power. The turn of this century found us living large and at the close of this decade I'm afraid we'll still be digging out from the combinations of the stock market crash, the Internet bust and the burst real estate bubble. If we keep letting the grownups run the world, I'm afraid there won't be much of it left to run by the time we take over.

But if we start now, you and me and my friends and your friends and our classmates and younger brothers and little sisters and their friends and their classmates, one by one we can pick a cause, solve it a little bit at a time and change the world we live in.

YOU CAN'T JOIN THE MOVEMENT IF YOU DON'T MOVE!

It's not just we revolutionaries who will wage the battle. Take a page from Jasmine's book and think of everyone we help along the way; they can be new recruits as well. I always end my *Just Yell Fire* training sessions by encouraging girls to tell two friends what they've just learned, and to tell those girls to tell two friends, and so on and so on.

So even the girls who don't come to see me personally can download the video, print the teacher's guide and learn the ten measures to save their lives and avoid abduction. They can even teach a class on their own; church groups and Girl Scouts and PE classes write me all the time to tell me how well they did teaching the class for the first time – and how they can't wait to do it again!

You and I, we're part of a movement now; what we do doesn't just affect one or two people but everyone those one or two people come into contact with hereafter. The gifts we give and the time we spend and the money we donate, these offerings go out into the world and come back to us tenfold.

Dallas and Reverend Cecil Williams in Washington, DC

We *can* change the world, one revolution at a time.

By reading this book, you've already declared war against apathy, laziness and the status quo. Now it's time to light the fuse and start your revolution for real. And don't forget to send me news from the front line. Go to **www.justyellfire.com** for my address or my email address.

I can't wait to hear from you!

■

Why do you think I wrote this book? I knew I couldn't change the world all by myself, so I decided to recruit a few million volunteers, one reader at a time. You do what you do, I'll do what I do, and if we stick together, we can change the course of history.

■

DALLAS JESSUP, 17

Founder & Spokesperson — Just Yell Fire, Inc.
A non-profit Empowering Girls in 42 countries

Dallas Jessup has accomplished more in her 17 years than most people do in a lifetime. When she discovered that 1 in 4 young women are victims of sexual assault and that there are 114,000 attempted abductions each year in the U.S. alone, this black belt street-fighting instructor decided to turn the tables on predators.

At 14 she wrote, co-produced, and starred in the film *Just Yell Fire*, which teaches girls ages 11 to 19 a Dating Bill of Rights and get-away strategies for date rape or other attack situations. She put *Just Yell Fire* online for FREE and founded a non-profit to distribute the film to schools, shelters, and teens at no cost. The results – 600,000 downloads and DVDs given away in 41 countries. The film was 1 of the 10 most downloaded worldwide in 2007 and earned the American Library Association's "most notable video" in 2008.

To raise awareness of the plight of high school and college women she travels 10,000 miles a month speaking at schools, womens' conferences, shelters, and law enforcement events while still attending Portland, Oregon's prestigious St. Mary's Academy. Dallas was the youngest keynote speaker ever at an annual national Mensa convention, is a 2008 Teen Choice Awards nominee, and speaks regularly at FBI events and conferences.

Jessup toured India speaking at a dozen high schools and universities in response to a plea to her, as America's top teen safety advocate, to take on the international sex trafficking crisis where girls are abducted and sold as slaves. She now uses web-based technology to do video conferences for young women in countries as far away as Pakistan.

Dallas was inducted into the National Caring Hall of Fame in Washington, DC, and has been recognized by dozens of organizations as a Teen Hero for her work. She has appeared on many national television shows, in a dozen national magazines, on radio stations, and in newspapers across the United States

Dallas Jessup, a high school senior at 16, continues to operate the *Just Yell Fire* non-profit and tours the country sharing her *Just Yell Fire* teen-safety campaign for girls and young women, as well as inspiring high school and college students to create their own revolution of community service as well as . She will begin college in the fall of 2009.

To learn more about Dallas Jessup
and how you can make a difference visit:

www.youngrevolutionarieswhorock.com

www.justyellfire.com